Steve Mizerak's

PLAY BETTER POOL

STEVE MIZERAK'S

PLAY BETTER POOL

WINNING TECHNIQUES AND STRATEGIES FOR MASTERING THE GAME

STEVE MIZERAK WITH
MICHAEL E. PANOZZO
AND GEORGE FELS

CONTEMPORARY BOOKS
A TRIBUNE COMPANY

Library of Congress Cataloging-in-Publication Data

Mizerak, Steve, 1944–
    Steve Mizerak's play better pool: winning techniques and strategies for
mastering the game / Steve Mizerak with Michael E. Panozzo.
        p.   cm.
    ISBN 0-8092-3427-0
    1. Pool (Game)   I. Panozzo, Michael E.   II. Title.
GV891.M6926   1996
794.7′3—dc20   96-15163
                                                                   CIP

Cover design by Laurie Liebewein
Interior design by Mary Lockwood
Photos by Gerry Corbato

Published by Contemporary Books
An imprint of NTC/Contemporary Publishing Company
Two Prudential Plaza, Chicago, Illinois 60601-6790
Manufactured in the United States of America
International Standard Book Number: 0-8092-3427-0
10   9   8   7   6   5   4   3   2   1

Contents

Introduction

Pool is one of those games that people seem to insist on making harder for themselves.

By rights, it should be a reasonably easy game to learn. After all, no particular strength is required, nor is it even desirable; this is a game of finesse. No one is allowed to block or tackle you to prevent you from getting to the balls. No one can move the balls to make them harder for you to hit. The only physical motion required to execute a proper stroke is restricted to your stroking forearm and your eyeballs. And all you have to do is roll a 5-ounce ball a few feet, often a few inches, over smooth, level cloth.

So why aren't you playing better pool? Probably because you're introducing some less-than-ideal habits to your stroking and/or aiming fundamentals. The good news is that because pool requires so little of you physically, you can make some terrific improvements merely by improving those same fundamentals. At the same time, you can probably improve the way you approach pool mentally. After all, this is mostly a mental game.

With this book, you've come to the right place to improve both your fundamentals and your mental game. We'll take a good look at common problem areas—and the proper approach to them—in the basics and the three most popular pool games. With reasonable practice, and a bit of mental discipline, you should see improvements almost immediately.

One of the things that make pool so magical is that you can *continue* to improve at it for most of your life! I've been at it for over 40 years—I started at age 4—and I still learn something new almost every time I come to the table. If you go about it the right way, even a good practice session can add to your knowledge, enthusiasm, and ability.

As enjoyable as pool is to play recreationally, it's even more fun to play really well. Let's get started on improving your game. First we'll consider problem areas and common errors players make; then we'll talk about the proper approach to each.

STEVE MIZERAK'S

PLAY BETTER POOL

1

◉ The Basics ◉

Far too many players make the assumption that the keys to playing better pool revolve around the game's many subtleties—advanced position play, analysis of the layout of balls on the table, learning complicated patterns, etc.

As the saying goes, *it ain't necessarily so*.

While becoming a student of the advanced game will certainly help you become a better player, you won't get very far without first becoming a better player at the fundamental level. Bad habits and flaws in your stance, bridge, stroke, and aim need to be addressed and corrected before you try to move into a more sophisticated approach to the game. Adding components to your playing arsenal is a lot easier when the foundation of your game is solid.

Problem Areas

How Do You Stand?

Let's suppose you're a football player. Would you approach the scrimmage line indifferently, settle into a lazy crouch, and wait for the snap of the ball? You'd find yourself on your hindquarters in no time.

There's no risk of physical contact in pool—but that doesn't mean you can disregard a correct stance. Like just about every other sport I can think of, pool requires a proper stance if you're to hit the ball effectively. And the problem for a lot of pool beginners, and even intermediate players, is that they're not consistent about their stance. If you watch inexperienced players for any length of time, you might see them in five or six different stances during the same game!

This is a very common error in stance. I'm standing far too erect, which makes aiming with accuracy a lot tougher.

Conversely, in this photo I'm too low over the cue to be comfortable. Many beginners and intermediate players think that if they get right down over the cue stick, their aim will be more accurate. Not necessarily true. Remember, you must be comfortable when you're shooting.

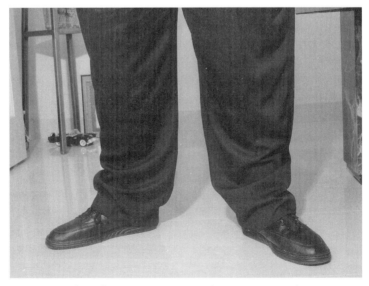

Yet another all-too-common mistake is improper placement of the feet. Here they're not spaced properly.

I'm out of balance here. My body is way over to one side and I'm leaning over the cue. Terrible.

In this instance, my chin isn't over the cue. That means my line of sight isn't in line with the cue either.

Here's the total disaster package! My feet aren't spaced properly, I'm out of balance, and I'm too far from the table. You name it, I'm doing it wrong!

An effective stance at the pool table includes balance, comfort, and consistency. That means you should stand the same way for nearly every shot. If the game you're playing requires you to blast the balls open on the break, as in Eight-Ball and Nine-Ball, then it's OK to stand slightly more erect for your break. (We'll take a closer look at why you do that later on in the book.) Otherwise, resist the temptation to take up your stance lazily; use a consistent stance, even on the very easiest shots. That kind of mental discipline will help you conquer pool's pressure situations.

Where do most players go wrong in their stances? Most commonly, it's in the placement of their feet—in standing too straight or bending over too far; in the position of their bodies in relation to the shot; and in the placement of their heads in relation to the cue. There are some other flaws that can crop up, but those are the biggies. A correct pool stance should feel *good* to you. If it doesn't, you're going to be distracted mentally, which just about obliterates your chances of successful execution. Remember, this is a highly mental game.

But on the positive side, your improved stance will usually elevate your game all by itself. Not only will you be more relaxed mentally, but also you'll have made it easier for yourself to hit the cue ball as you'd like to. In pool, the only things you really have direct control over are (1) your body and (2) your cue. You have some indirect control over the cue ball, and none whatsoever over the object balls—even though you do see lots of players bending, twisting, and making horrible faces, trying to wish an object ball into a pocket. None of that works.

Your Bridge over Troubled Waters

What the incredibly complex game of pool boils down to is this: can you bring your cue forward, in a perfectly straight line, to hit the cue ball exactly where you intend to? Once you can do that, most of the game's other aspects automatically begin to fall into place. (We'll be covering stroke next—but first things first.)

Your cue needs to be *guided* into that straight line. And that's where your bridge hand comes in. A good solid bridge controls the top half of your cue—the shaft—allowing it to come forward smoothly, in a straight line, without wobbling. Also, your correct bridge will help you keep your cue level (that's a must) and strike the cue ball where you intend to. Most of the time, it's your bridge hand you adjust—not your stroking hand—in order to hit the cue ball above or below its center.

There are several kinds of proper bridges, depending on exactly where the cue ball is; unfortunately, mistakes can be made in all of them. Common errors include leaving too much room for the cue to come through, not leaving *enough* room for the cue to come through, inappropriate bridging off a rail or over an interfering ball, and improper distance between the bridge hand and the cue ball. All will interfere with correct stroke production, and that's one of the most important factors holding players back.

Speaking of Strokes . . .

It's a motion of roughly 12 inches and not much more. How can such a compact striking action give so many players so much grief?

In *many* ways, that's how. Of all the games on this earth in which a ball is struck with something—even the human

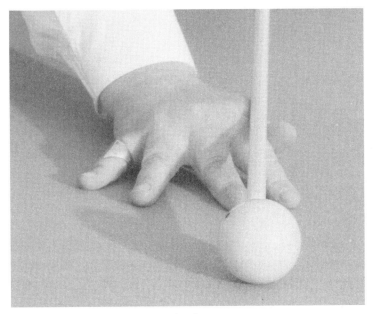

The open bridge. Easy and safe.

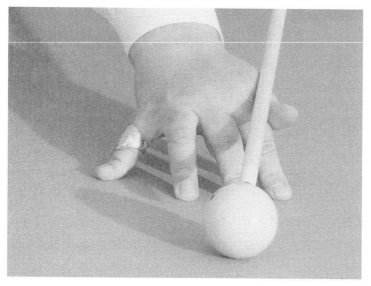

Simply lift the heel of your hand and you have the open bridge raised for follow shots.

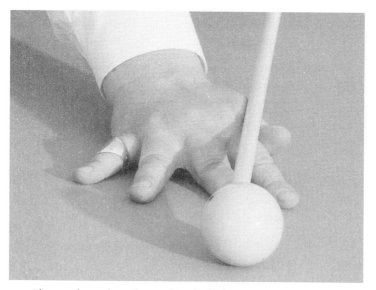

Flatten the palm of your hand all the way onto the table and you can lower the open bridge for draw shots.

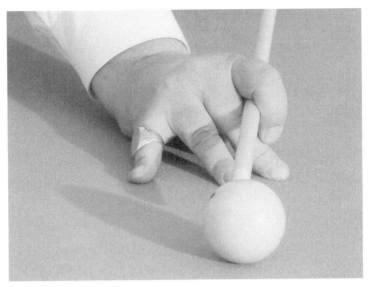

Notice the space in this closed bridge. This bridge is too wobbly.

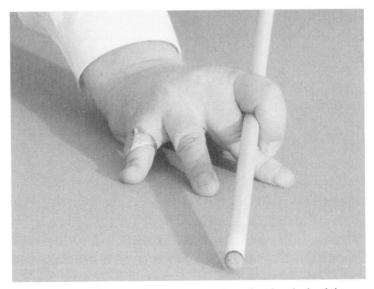

This bridge is too tight. It doesn't allow for the shaft of the cue to glide smoothly and effortlessly through the bridge.

It doesn't take much intelligence to figure out that a closed bridge up on the rail is awkward and inefficient. Don't use it!

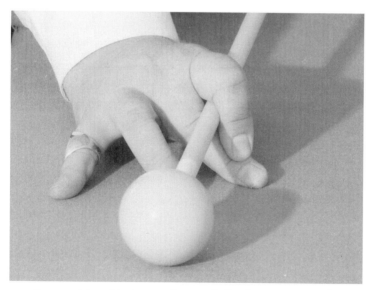

You must be able to see the cue ball when you aim. This bridge is way too short.

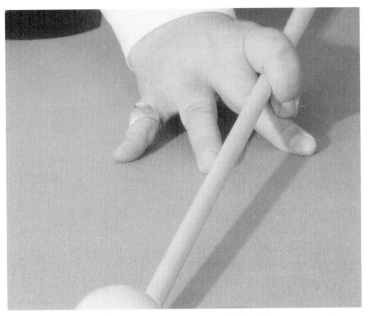

A bridge too far! It's going to be awfully difficult to maintain an accurate hit on the cue ball when the bridge is this far from the ball.

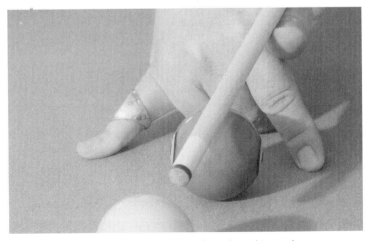

It may seem a bit awkward at first, but this is the proper way to bridge over an object ball. It's actually a lot more balanced and solid than it looks.

hand, as in handball or volleyball—none involves fewer dynamics than pool. The pool stroke is so simple, in fact, that hardly anybody can do it.

Here, in no special order, are just a few of the things that can and do go wrong with strokes:

- Using too much arm motion. The simplicity of a pool stroke fools a lot of players into thinking that if they don't complicate it, they won't be doing enough.

- Holding the stroking arm too far out from the body or too close. Either one will make it just about impossible to bring the cue forward in that straight line I mentioned.

- Having too tight a grip on the cue. This is usually caused by the pressure of competition. It's impossible to produce a fluid, smooth stroke if you're clenching the cue in your rear hand. In fact, it's impossible to be fluid or smooth at *anything* if you're tightened up.

- Swerving the cue one way or the other by trying to steer the ball instead of creating that straight line.

- Elevating the back end of your cue instead of keeping it level with the table surface.

- Using too much, or too little, wrist action.

- Rushing into your shot. This is frequently due to the game's pressures.

- Having too short a backswing. Or, too short a follow-through. And frequently both.

- Overhitting. And underhitting.

● Taking too few practice strokes (and incorrectly executed, at that). Or too many.

● Bringing your head up out of your shooting stance too soon. Pool is not dissimilar to golf: you attack an inert white ball on a green surface; it's just you and that white ball, with no opponent to interfere with your stroke—and you have to keep your head down in both games.

Take a look behind you every once in a while. You may notice things—like the fact that the cue is too far from your body!

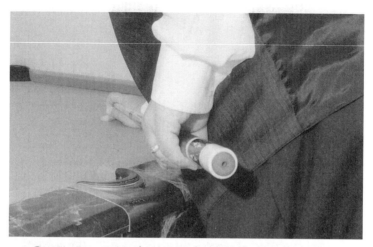

Or you may notice that you're holding the cue too close to your body. Not very comfortable, is it?

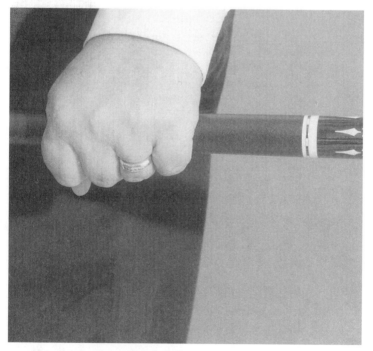

This death grip will only kill your stroke. Lighten up!

Don't jack up your cue like this unless you must. You sacrifice a lot of accuracy and control with this approach.

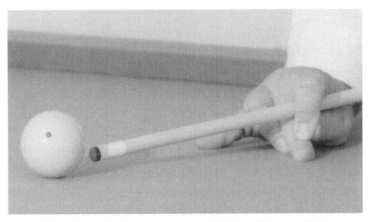

Follow-through is so important. Don't sell yourself short with this kind of follow-through.

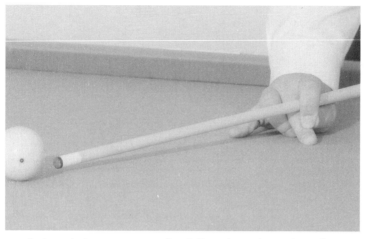

It doesn't do you any good to follow through too far either.

No matter how critical the shot, don't let pressure make you rear up.

Aiming to Please

Even on the shortest putts, good golfers will examine a shot from a 360-degree vantage. That's because each green is different, with rolls of its own; none is flat or predictable.

That's not necessary in pool, because the playing surface is smooth and level (in theory, anyway). Your view of your shot from in back of the cue ball should suffice to prepare you for a successful execution. And yet many players—including some very good ones—don't really know what they're aiming at.

▽ Are you *guessing* at what you have to do to make your shot? In that case, I know about 500 players who will be delighted to pay your cab fare, both ways, if you'll agree to play them.

▽ Are you trying to "see" the actual point of contact on the object ball? That's a good way to go blind. Or nuts. When two spheres of equal size collide, the actual area of contact is about the size of a pinpoint.

▽ Are you falling for that old bromide about "Aim the center of the cue ball at the point of contact"? You'll be lucky to get the object ball within 6 inches of its target.

▽ Are you hitting the cue ball in its center? If you're putting side-spin of one kind or the other on the ball—intentionally or not—that has to be compensated for in your aiming; otherwise you can expect a miss.

But don't despair. There's some good news here too: once you've learned how to aim properly, in no time at all you'll be able to do that as well as the world's great players do. That's because aiming, in and of itself, is really a very simple matter—even if it bewilders you now.

Putting a New Spin on Things

Exactly where on that cue ball are you? By that, I mean where do you intend to strike the cue ball? In its exact center? Above or below the center? To the left or right of it? Above or below *and* to the left or right of center? As I said earlier, your success at pool comes down to your ability to hit the cue ball exactly where you plan to. Any deviation from that can't help but affect your shot. A cue ball is 2¼ inches in diameter; your cue tip is only 12 to 13 millimeters. So if you strike that cue ball anyplace except in its center, it's going to *deflect* to some extent off your cue tip. After that, the spin you've imparted is going to make the cue ball curve slightly. And when that spinning, curving cue ball contacts an object ball, it's going to transfer some of that spin and alter the object ball's path too. (All that, just because you missed your point of aim on the cue ball by a few measly millimeters!)

As you might guess, failing to strike the cue ball in its center is at the heart of many beginners' mistakes. The catch is that situations are going to come up, in all forms of pool, where you *have* to hit the cue ball high or low, and/or with some left or right English.

How can your cueing the ball go wrong? Let me count the ways:

- You don't know where it is you want to strike the cue ball.

- Your bridge may not be firm enough, allowing the cue to deviate from that straight-line delivery you want.

- Your stroking arm is too far from, or too close to, your body. I know I mentioned this in discussing stance, but it can be a negative factor in your cueing the ball, too.

● Your stance doesn't align you correctly with your shot. As the computer hotshots say: Garbage in, garbage out.

● Your cue isn't level at the moment of contact. A cue ball struck with an elevated cue behaves differently than one struck with a level cue.

"There's many a slip 'twixt the cup and the lip," the old saying goes, and the same is true for what can happen in the time between when you aim a pool shot and when you actually shoot.

What Shape Are You In?

I'm not talking about your physical condition. "Shape" is how quite a few pool players refer to position play, the manner in which you select and plan for the shot(s) you will take after you make the one immediately in front of you.

After all, pool only requires you to sink one ball and send the cue ball to a place advantageous to sinking another one. If you could do that in every single turn, you'd be able to beat me and every other player in the universe. There has never been anyone who could do that every single time, of course, and there never will be. But no single aspect of pool bamboozles beginners—and frequently much more experienced players as well—like position play.

▽ Are you thinking ahead far enough? Remember, pocketing a single ball doesn't mean much unless that lone ball is all you need to win.

▽ Do you have a reasonable idea of which ball you *should* be playing for next?

▽ Do you hit the cue ball too hard? If so, you won't be as good as you could be at predicting where it will end up.

▽ Do you put English, or side-spin, on the cue ball when you don't need to? Then you're making your position play far harder than it has to be.

▽ Are you knocking multiple object balls around unnecessarily? A player once told me, "When I was young, I moved as many balls as possible on each shot, to keep from looking bad when I missed." He'll probably never know just how dumb he did look. The vast majority of all pool shots should move just two balls: the cue ball and the object ball you want to sink.

▽ Are you sending the cue ball off more rails than you need to? As a great poet said once, "Simplicity is genius."

Are You Afraid of a 2¼-Inch Ball?

Probably not—until you get into a pool game you really want to win. At that point, it's just about certain that shots are going to come up that intimidate you for some reason or other. It would be great if all the game ever asked you to do was shoot at balls right in front of holes, but that's not the way pool goes.

What makes a "hard" shot in pool? There are probably as many answers as people you ask for an opinion, but let's look at it like this: shots that offer you a less-frontal view of your desired point of contact on the object ball (in other words, the thinner cut shots), shots with more distance between cue ball and object ball, and shots in which the object ball must be sent some distance diagonally all qualify as difficult for most players. After that, it's pretty subjective; some players hate shooting object balls on or near a rail, especially when they have an acute angle to overcome, and some play-ers are even terrified of shots that are dead straight in!

Players who let those feelings seep into their game are making multiple mistakes by doing so. Why think of the shots as "hard" in the first place? They're just shots, and they are makeable. Negative thinking can do nothing but hold back your progress in general. And if you're rearranging your posi-tion sequences just to avoid a shot you don't like, you're hold-ing yourself back from playing better pool.

Solutions

Now that I've outlined the potential problems in your game, it's time to discuss some possible solutions.

Stance

If you had to boil all instruction on pool stance down to a sin-gle sentence, it would probably be this: stand in a way that's comfortable for you.

Here's a good stance—comfortable and balanced.

Here are a few more stance variations. Even when you need to stretch, it's possible to maintain a comfortable, balanced stance.

It sounds simple, yet you see guys playing in stances that can't *possibly* be comfortable. They're not balanced, and that means they can't hit the ball as they'd like to.

All a successful pool stance really demands is comfort, balance, and your chin over the cue. Comfort is something you determine for yourself. As for balance, your feet should be placed in the same direction—not angled—and your weight should be evenly distributed, to the point where you could resist a shove on your shooting side. It's usually a good idea to bend your front knee slightly on most shots, depending on how you're built and where your center of gravity is.

Your body should probably be closer to the table than the butt of your cue, and angled away from your shot—about 45 degrees—to let your shooting arm swing freely and clear your hip. But there are no set rules as to how far from the table your body should be; that all depends on cue ball location and, again, what's comfortable for you. Just make sure you're neither cramped for room nor reaching for shots. Some shots require you to stand on your toes, or even lie out over the table, but your stance must still involve balance. Never pull the trigger on any shot where you don't feel comfortable and balanced.

Don't do this. Now you're unreasonably stretched for the shots.

One of the problems inherent in standing too erect is that you tend to put too much pressure directly down on the bridge hand.

If your arm isn't swinging freely, you're not standing correctly; it's just that simple. Your correct stance will give you the optimal view of the cue ball plus optimal swinging room. Equally important, your stance will key the other elements of your stroke mechanics to work smoothly and in unison.

How low your head should be over the cue is, again, a matter of personal preference. Some top players actually touch their cues with their chins; others stand almost upright. That decision has to do with what's comfortable, your height, your reach, and your flexibility, especially in the back muscles. I stand with my chin about 8 inches over the cue; the great Willie Mosconi did too. In general, standing lower makes more sense than standing straighter. But in determining where you're most comfortable, try starting out with your head 12 inches over the cue, and adjust from there.

Here's another good tip for your stance: while your pool stance is similar to the three-point stance of a football player,

Don't hold your cue butt too close to your chin.

don't put too much pressure on your bridge hand by leaning on it. Not only will you be uncomfortable, but you'll also be making it harder to maintain a bridge that your cue can come through smoothly.

The reason it's OK to stand up a bit straighter when breaking the balls open in Eight-Ball or Nine-Ball is that you can then get more of your body behind your stroke, and those are the two occasions in pool when a bit more power is desirable.

But aside from those breaks, the most important single aspect of your stance is that you get into it as consistently as you can (except when you're stretching), even on the simplest shots. Once you know your stance is correct each time, you've got one less thing to worry about . . . and that can be a valuable edge.

Learn to shoot easy shots with either hand. It will come in handy more often than you imagine.

Rest the mechanical bridge on the table and point the butt of your cue at your chest—no higher.

When a shot is beyond your reach, you have two options: shoot it in opposite-handed, or use the mechanical bridge. Do *not* grip your cue at its very end, bridge 18 inches, and shoot it "out of your belly," no matter how simple the shot seems. I strongly suggest you practice shooting a few simple shots opposite-handed each time you're at the table alone. If you're

Don't lift the mechanical bridge!

more comfortable with the mechanical bridge, remember that its nonbusiness end belongs on the table surface, not in the air with your stroking hand. Set it in place, flat on the table, and brace it with your bridge hand. Bend forward slightly, and sight down the shaft of your cue. Try to keep the head of the bridge about 12 inches from the cue ball.

Bridge

How far from the cue ball should your bridge hand be? In most instances, approximately 8 to 10 inches—except that your table layout may not always permit you to put your hand

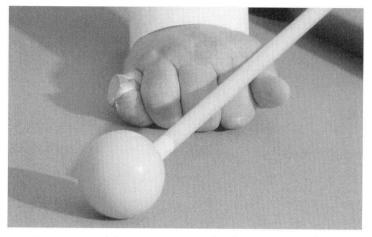

Here's a good four-step process for forming your closed bridge. First make a fist.

down where you like to. Also, experienced players adjust the length of their bridges, shortening up when they want to minimize cue-ball movement after contact, lengthening out when they want a longer stroke and more action for cue-ball travel. But until you're satisfied that your stroke is perfectly straight, stick with that 8- to 10-inch distance.

Don't be intimidated by how many different bridges there seem to be to learn. The very first bridge you probably learned—the five-finger open bridge—can accompany you all the way to the peak of your game. After all, that's just about the only bridge that snooker players use, and they're the world's best shot makers by far, firing the cue games' smallest balls into pockets barely one ball wide across a 6′ × 12′ table! The only real disadvantage of this bridge is that you have less control of your cue. The pressures of a game, or your need to add speed or spin to the cue ball, can make your cue fly right off your bridge. But if you can discipline yourself not to do that, this is a valuable bridge itself *and* it serves as a good stepping-stone to other things. So don't dismiss it

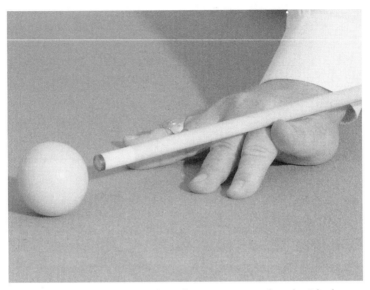

After you make a fist, then flatten out your hand with the cue still running between your thumb and index finger.

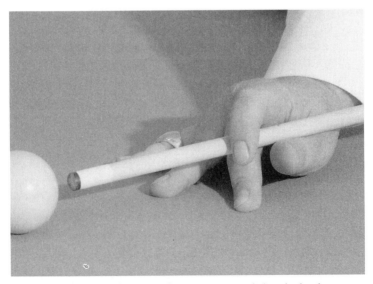

Lift your index finger and wrap it around the shaft of the cue.

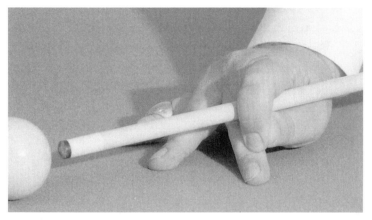

Raise your knuckles slightly and spread your fingers for more balance.

as being for beginners only. Once you've learned how to cup your bridge hand to hit higher on the cue ball, and spread it out to hit lower, this bridge should be a permanent part of your game.

For added control, though, and to use more speed in your stroke, the closed bridge should be the next one you learn. Forming the bridge is pretty easy—but a lot of players have trouble getting comfortable with it unless they play at least once a week. Assuming you're going to play that much and hopefully more, you have to have this bridge. It's the bridge used by all professional players, and it allows you to control your cue better, which in turn means you control the cue ball better. Any time you need to add something to the cue ball's natural roll—speed, spin on either side, or draw—you want the added control of the closed bridge.

To form this bridge, make a loop of your index finger and thumb. Place that loop alongside the knuckle of your middle finger. You should be able to slide the shaft of your cue smoothly through that loop—but remember, in a straight line. If your loop is too big, the cue will wobble. Keep the heel

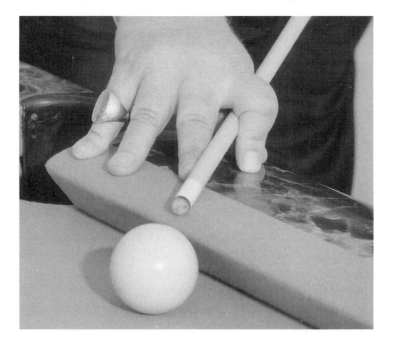

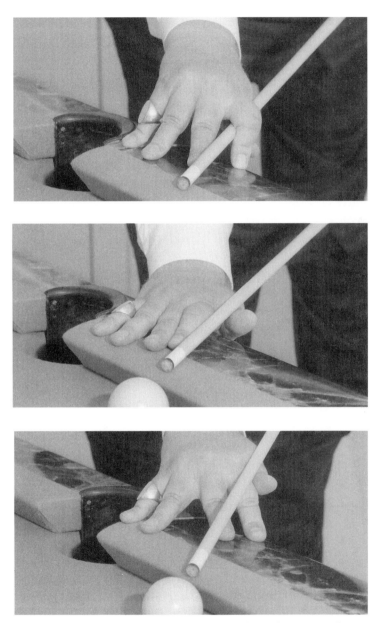

Shooting off the rail is strictly a matter of comfort. Just make sure you can keep the cue straight. It's almost always best if you can slide the cue on the rail, keeping it as parallel to the table bed as possible.

of your hand, and your bottom three fingers, on the table; that's the solid base your bridge needs.

If the cue ball rests on or near a rail, though, you can't use the closed bridge anymore, because the cue ball will be obscured from your view. The easiest rail bridge to form and learn is one where you tuck your thumb beneath your palm, letting the cue glide between your index and middle fingers. That's the ideal bridge to use when you're shooting away from the rail. Another option is to bring back your old friend the flat open bridge—but in that case, you'll want to rest your thumb on the rail and lift the heel of your hand slightly. The V groove between your thumb and index finger is now formed at rail height. Remember to keep your cue level!

When you're shooting *along* a rail instead of away from it, bridging becomes more difficult. The bridge to use in this instance is kind of a cousin to the rail bridge described in the preceding paragraph; the cue still glides between your index and middle fingers—but this time wrap your index finger over the edge of the rail. That will give you added stability and control.

If your obstacle to bridging is not a rail but an interfering object ball, go back to your flat open bridge, but fold your index finger under (so you won't risk touching any balls with it) and raise your bridge so only your last three fingertips are in contact with the table surface. Your cue slides over the same V groove it always does. Again, you want all the firmness and stability you can manage—but don't bear down too hard on this bridge because its base is the weakest part of your hand.

Stroke

Like just about every other sport I can think of in which you hit a ball with something, a pool stroke should have a definite beginning, middle, and end. That means it should include a backswing, a fluid, unforced delivery, and a follow-through.

As logical as that sounds, many beginners and even some better players eliminate the beginning or the end of their strokes, and sometimes both. The result is a hurried "poke" that pushes the ball forward without any real control, power, or accuracy. Don't do that! A successful pool stroke is often referred to as a pendulum, because that's the action your stroking arm should simulate. Your arm comes forward naturally, moving only from the elbow down, and that's all you really need to propel the cue ball; pool requires very little strength. If you're holding your cue at the right point, your stroking arm should be straight up and down—in other words, exactly perpendicular to the floor—at the moment your cue contacts the cue ball. That will also help ensure that the cue is neither too close to nor too far from your body.

How long should your backswing be? Just a little less than the length of your bridge (after all, you don't want to pull your cue tip back through the loop in your bridge). If you're gripping the cue correctly—not too loose, and especially not too tight—it will automatically be straight for your backswing. But if you're choking your stick, your wrist will tend to turn and bring your cue forward in something other than a straight line. It's only your thumb and first two fingers that really count in your grip; your ring finger and pinky more or less come along for the ride. Leave a little space between your palm and the cue—which should open up slightly on your backswing. On your follow-through, your palm should come down on the cue, but that doesn't mean you tighten your grip. By all means, remind yourself to check on your grip when you're in tough situations. If it's correct, many of your other fundamentals will fall into place automatically.

But before you even get to your backswing, remember to take some practice strokes, just as golfers and even baseball players do. Practice strokes accomplish more than you think; they help you establish your stroking and playing rhythm (*very* important), lock in your aim, and check all your funda-

Perfect delivery! Notice that the back hand is perpendicular to the table at the point of contact with the cue ball.

mentals before firing. It's a good idea to take the same number of practice strokes each time, whatever your preferred number is. If you don't take enough, you may rush your shot, and then you won't reap all the benefits just mentioned. If you take too many, you're going to create pressure for yourself, which could ruin your concentration. Many expert players take three to five practice strokes, but there's no one perfect number. The important things are to relax, and to aim at the exact point on the cue ball you want to hit. Make sure the tightness of your grip, the movement of your lower arm, the accuracy of your aim, and the fluidity of your stroke all feel and look ideal to you. If not, stand up straight and make whatever adjustments it takes to feel right. Don't do that while you're still in your stance; most of the time, that won't work. If everything feels and looks perfect, pull the trigger!

Some players have perfected their stroke deliveries by practicing stroking into an empty pop bottle, or through the handle on a coffee cup, without touching the sides. Others stroke an imaginary ball with their cues lined up parallel to a rail, to check the straightness of their follow-through and the

A good backswing will bring the cue tip right into your bridge hand.

position of their arms and elbows. An even easier method is to practice stroking the cue ball off either the head spot or foot spot of the table. If your stroke and/or follow-through aren't straight, the spot will tattle on you every single time. Try this exercise by striking the cue ball in its center at first, then with spin to either side.

What about *after* cue-ball contact? There are just as many players who forget to follow through as those who forget a good efficient backswing. And that's too bad because a follow-through is one of the most important elements of your stroke. Again, in any other game in which you strike a ball, players are taught to *accelerate through the ball,* and that's true in pool too. The tip of your cue should go straight through the cue ball and follow it about 8 inches. Start right now to discipline yourself to keep your head down, all the way through your follow-through. Don't give in to the temptation to jump up and watch where the balls are going. In fact, it's a good idea to stay down in your stance longer than necessary, while you're teaching yourself this very good habit. The importance of keeping your head down simply can't be overstated.

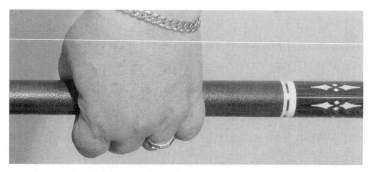

A couple of things to look for when you stroke: Don't turn your wrist in!

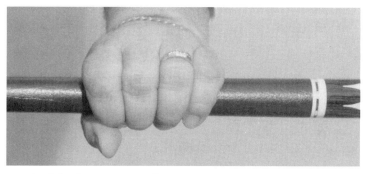

And don't turn your wrist out.

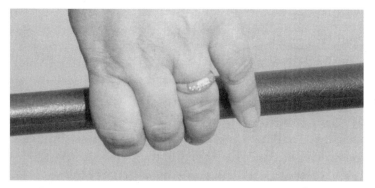

The proper grip can be made by wrapping only the first three fingers around the butt. Keeping your little finger loose will ensure that you're not gripping the cue too tightly.

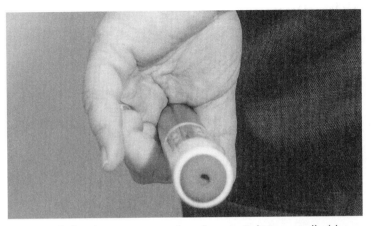

From behind, you can see that the cue is being cradled by the fingers only. The palm of the hand is not wrapped around the cue.

Aiming

OK, so you're hitting the cue ball exactly as you'd like to. Now where do you want to strike the object ball?

What most amateurs or beginners do is use their cues to "point" at the pocket, through the object ball; some even lay their cues on the table to determine the correct point of aim on the ball. The catch is, that's not quite aiming. Because so many beginning players try to hit the cue ball dead center on practically all their shots, they fall into the habit of aiming the center of the cue ball at the desired spot on the object ball— and that just won't work, except when the cue ball, object ball, and pocket are all in a straight line.

So forget about finding an aiming point for the center of the cue ball, and concentrate instead on *how much of the cue ball* will strike the object ball. When you have to cut a ball really thin, for instance, one way to aim would be to concentrate on having the edge of your cue ball contact the edge of the object ball. If the object ball is to be cut at approximately a 45-degree angle, you might try aiming the center of the cue

A good follow-through will deliver the cue tip right to the cloth. Notice that the cue tip has not come up, and neither has the butt.

ball at the edge of the object ball (this is the so-called half-ball hit, although in reality you're striking one quarter of the ball, not one half). But if you keep aiming that cue-ball center at the object ball regardless of how your specific shot lies, you're not going to enjoy much success.

In fact, the aiming success you do enjoy is going to be a product of your hand/eye coordination, and since that gift varies from one individual to the next, the aiming devices you develop for yourself are largely a matter of what works for you. One excellent proven method is to begin gauging your aim by practicing straight shots, then moving the cue ball a few inches to one side or the other to create slight angles, then more severe angles. Focus both on how your aim changes each time the shot does and on the *feel* of the shot. Straight-in shots, with their solid contact, feel quite a bit different from shots where you're clipping the edge of a ball. Shots where you spin the cue ball to one side or the other feel different from shots where you cue the ball in its vertical center. And you should

Contrary to what far too many players do, the ritual of pointing the object ball at the pocket isn't really aiming.

be aware of all those different feelings; they will actually improve your aim.

But however you choose to develop your aiming skills, here's a valuable tip: the right time to begin aiming a pool shot is before you even lean forward to assume your shooting stance. Place your *chin* directly on the line between cue ball and object ball before you bend down. The reason for this emphasis is that when you're in your stance you always want your head directly over the cue. This important first step helps make sure that's exactly where it will be.

Cueing

Your shot isn't over when the object ball disappears into a hole—far from it. In fact, the most important part of the whole game is where the cue ball goes after it strikes the object ball you wanted it to.

Correct stance, bridge, aim, and stroke must all be mastered if you're going to have any accuracy on your shots. But remember, sinking a single ball doesn't mean very much in pool, unless that one ball is all you need to win the game. You become a good pool player by learning what you have to do to make shots consecutively, and keeping your opponent in the chair.

There are five basic ways to cue the ball: dead in its center (fine for practice but actually pretty rare in competition), above its center (or "follow"), below its center (or "draw"), and to either side of center. And shots often require you to cue the ball above or below center with side-spin, or English, too.

In fact, the only time in pool when you want to hit your cue ball in its exact middle—assuming you *can* do that, and many players can't—is when you have a shot that lies straight-in to a pocket, the cue ball is only a foot or so from the object ball, and you want the cue ball to stop in its tracks upon contact. For that shot, a center-ball hit and a moderate stroke will get the job done. But how many such shots do you see in a typical game? If the object ball is any farther from the cue ball than that, and you still want to stop the cue ball dead (and remember, you can do that only on straight shots), you're going to have to hit it below its center. That's because a cue ball can only stop in its track if it has no spin on it at the moment it contacts the object ball. When you strike it in its exact center, you send it on its way in a *skid,* with no spin at all, before it begins to roll naturally. But, depending on how hard you hit it, it won't skid very long. If it's rolling when it strikes the object ball, it won't stop. (You can demonstrate this for yourself by substituting one of the striped balls for the cue ball, cueing it as you like, and observing the results—but if you play in a commercial room, the owner might not appreciate your cueing an object ball.)

When your shot is straight-in, then, your cue ball can do one of just three things: stop dead, follow after the object ball, or come back toward you. Of those three, follow shots are probably the easiest on which to gauge where your cue ball will go. How far the cue ball follows after the object ball depends entirely on how high and how hard you strike the cue ball. (Don't hit it any higher than three quarters of the way up the ball, by the way; there's too much risk of miscueing.) A good way to learn the follow shot is to set up a straight-in shot, and practice achieving various follow distances; say, 12 inches at first, then 24 (or whatever intervals feel comfort-able to you), then coming as close as you can to following the ball into a pocket. Mark where your cue ball ends up each time, using a cube of chalk, and soon you'll develop a feel for how hard to stroke the cue ball to achieve a given amount of follow.

Learning to draw the cue ball effectively is much harder for many beginners. All too often they assume the cue ball must be struck harder, and that simply isn't true. What's needed are a level cue and fluidity in your stroke, nothing more. The other common error, and one for you to begin avoiding immediately, is failure to strike the cue ball low enough. A cue ball must be struck well below its center—*at least* three quarters of the way down the ball—to create draw. That means lowering your bridge hand as much as possible, no matter what kind of bridge you're using, so your cue will be level with the contact point on the cue ball. (When your cue ball is on or near a rail, you'll have to elevate your cue to draw the ball, and, accordingly, shorten your follow-through.) You should be using your closed bridge for draw shots, by the way; only the best players can strike a controlled draw shot using the open bridge.

Putting English on the cue ball—in other words, striking it to the right or left of its vertical center—is something you should not attempt to add to your game until you're confident of your fundamentals. But it's still a part of the game that every player should be familiar with. While it does complicate your shots (after all, it introduces cue-ball deflection, curve, *and* spin at the same time), it also will offer you advantages during a game that mere center cue ball, follow, or draw will not. If you need to change the angle at which your cue ball comes off a cushion, or avoid running into another object ball after striking the one you want, you may have to introduce some English into the shot.

But first you'll have to understand the potential of side-spin. Practice some shots, even some very easy ones, hitting the cue ball to one side or the other, and you'll quickly see that you can't aim your shots the same way you would if you were hitting the cue ball in its center. If you're hitting the cue ball on its right side, you should aim a bit farther to the right than you normally would, and vice versa when you cue the ball to its left. Also, remember that there's some friction between the cue ball and the object ball; a cue ball spinning to its right will "throw" the object ball slightly left, and again, vice versa.

Once you're aiming successfully—that is, once your shot-making skill and confidence are above average—by all means practice shots cueing the ball every available way. If one area of your practice turns up more misses than another, invest extra time there. But you've got to learn to convert off-center cue-ball hits to your advantage.

Position

If you are relatively new to pool, you can probably remember some of the very first shots—maybe even *the* first shot—you ever made. It's a neat feeling, isn't it? You've taken on unfamiliar physical exercises, geometry and physics, and conquered them all.

Wait'll you find out how good it feels to make a bunch of shots right in a row!

"Running the balls" is what separates good players from beginners. It's also the reason everybody agrees that pool is mostly a mental game. As in chess, you have to be able to think several moves ahead. But chess doesn't involve any *execution* of the move you plan. In pool, first you have to formulate a plan, and then you have to execute accordingly. And your plan will be one of, "Which ball(s) do I want to take off the table after the one I'm shooting now; and where do I want my cue ball to be to do that?"

Position play is mostly a matter of common sense, plus your own knowledge of, and confidence in, what you can make the cue ball do in the way of follow, draw, and/or spin. If you're playing Eight-Ball, the most balls you can play position for is eight (your seven solids or stripes plus the 8-ball). If the game is Nine-Ball, the next shot ahead of you will always be the next-lowest-numbered ball remaining. But in Straight Pool, any ball left up there is, theoretically, fair game for your next shot; and that's why it's the best game to teach you position play for all the others.

The first thing to learn about position play is that it's much easier when you leave yourself angled shots, as opposed to those that are straight-in. The latter group of shots basically offers you cue-ball options along the same straight line you began with. But a shot offering you an angle between cue ball, object ball, and pocket also offers you—again, in theory—a chance to get the cue ball almost anyplace on the table you choose, using the correct spin and speed. So the first secret of running balls is to try to leave yourself angled shots. Even a very slight angle is usually preferable to none.

One simple, efficient way to begin your grasp of position concepts is to roll two object balls out on the empty table, making sure they don't end up too close to each other. Then choose a cue-ball location that lets you (1) pocket the first ball easily, and (2) send the cue ball someplace where you can pocket the second easily too. When you can do that successfully 8 out of 10 times, add a third object ball to the drill, and so on.

Naturally, position-play techniques will vary according to what pool game you're playing. However, to be good at any one pool game—or all of them—you'll need to plan at least three shots ahead. Here are some generalities that will help you learn position:

The Rule of Tangents

Some people call this the 90-degree rule, too, but by any name it means this: if you strike your cue ball in its center, making it skid at first, and it's still skidding when it contacts an object ball, it will go 90 degrees from the object ball's path. (If the shot is straight-in, the cue ball will stop dead.)

If you strike your cue ball above its center, your cue ball will deflect *less* than 90 degrees from the object ball's path. (How much less depends on cue-ball speed.) On straight-in shots, naturally, the cue ball will follow after the object ball.

And if you draw your cue ball, so it's still spinning back toward you when it contacts an object ball, it will deflect *more* than 90 degrees. (On straight shots, it will come back toward you.)

Moving the Balls

Sometimes when it's your turn to shoot, there will be many balls that are pocketable, maybe even all of them. At other times, especially if you're competing with a good player, there will be few or even no shots available. But a good percentage of the time, the layout you face will have both open shots *and* clustered balls that can't be made anywhere unless they're separated first.

Your rule of thumb here is easy to remember but hard to do: *Don't let the cue ball run into balls that are already open* after sinking the ball you intended to. Even if you barely graze a secondary ball, it will alter your anticipated cue-ball position, and that could turn the whole game around.

On the other hand, if balls are clustered and must be separated for you to continue your run, try to solve those problems sooner rather than later. Which open balls offer you an opportunity to send your cue ball at that cluster after contact? (The rule of tangents can be a big help in deciding on such shots.) And where will you need to be, with your cue ball, to accomplish that?

But don't rush madly into pocketing some open balls without a plan for dealing with trouble areas ahead. The problems won't go away; in fact, they become bigger with every open ball you sink.

Keep It Simple

Pool being the hard game that it is (at least if you want to play well), it's only sensible to make things easy for yourself in position play. The game won't always offer you easy opportunities, naturally, but what good players set out to do is conquer the difficulties immediately before them and restore the rest of the layout facing them to something familiar, recognizable, and simple. That's why in a pool audience you frequently hear, "They make it look so *easy!*"

Here are two great exercises that should improve your position play almost at once.

▽ Roll the object balls out on the table so no two are touching, and see how many you can make without your cue ball touching any ball other than the one you sink.

▽ When you can make consistent runs keeping your cue ball in the clear, you're ready to promote yourself to something quite a bit harder. See how many you can run without sending your cue ball to a rail. Not only will this one help you develop your shooting touch, but it will improve your pool thinking too.

Difficult Shots

First, understand right now that you are not going to come to the table with every last ball sitting right in front of a hole, making it impossible to miss. That's a nice dream, all right, but that's simply not the nature of the game. Neither will you be able to position your cue ball for a cinch shot each time; the game itself will deny you the chance to do that, and besides, we're all human, subject to misjudgments and errors.

Next, you have to be honest with yourself about what you consider a hard shot. Exactly which shots are you unhappy to see come up? Thin cuts? Rail shots? Long shots? There's just no substitute for *practicing* the precise shots that give you trouble until you have an added degree of comfort with them. Concentrate on why they need to be aimed differently. Then focus on how the correct hit will feel, and set those shots up and practice them over and over and over. Your fear won't go away by itself.

Another good tip is this: if it's thin cut shots or rail shots that intimidate you, set those shots up, maintaining the tough angles—but move both cue ball and object ball closer to the pocket. The correct techniques for making such shots remain the same, but chances are good that the shorter distance will help you get comfortable with the shots fairly quickly. When that happens, start moving both balls farther from the pocket, keeping the angle constant. After all, assuming your table is perfectly level, sending an object ball one foot with accuracy is no different from sending it five or six feet, except for cue-ball speed. In fact, to aid their aiming and confidence, many good players make it a point to visualize the pocket closer to the object ball than it actually is.

2

● Straight Pool ●

The Rules

While the official *Rule Book of the Billiard Congress of America* goes on for pages and pages on Straight Pool, the very basic rules are probably simpler than those of any other pool game. Both Eight-Ball (the world's most popular pool game by far) and Nine-Ball restrict you as to which remaining balls on the table are playable. But in Straight Pool, you're permitted to try to shoot any ball you wish into any pocket you wish. Each ball you sink as intended is worth one point. In the few Straight Pool tournaments played today, games are usually to 125 or 150 points, but most recreational players play to 100 or fewer points.

As in every other form of pool, following cue ball–object ball contact, either the cue ball or an object ball must touch a rail if no balls are pocketed (except on the game's opening break, when at least two object balls and the cue ball must all be driven to a rail). Although Straight Pool is sometimes called

A common mistake: I hit the rack too hard on the opening break and separated way too many balls.

Call Shot or Call Ball, you only have to announce the shots that aren't immediately obvious. Once it's understood which ball and pocket are intended, any way you get it there counts, even if it runs into three rails and six more balls on the way. If you're successful at that, any other balls that fall on the same shot count too.

Straight Pool is most often referred to as 14.1, because after 14 of the 15 balls have been pocketed, those 14 are reracked, with the spot where the head ball in the rack would usually go left vacant. So good players will try to leave that fifteenth ball someplace where it can be sunk *and* the cue ball sent toward that 14-ball rack to knock some more balls loose for more shots.

Problem Areas

The principal problem for all Straight Pool players, from beginners to champions, is missing shots. But there isn't much

Here's what happens when you hit the opening break perfectly.

I can do for you there, except to encourage you to develop your shot-making skills and confidence, through practice and competition, as much as you can. And after you've done that, keep in mind that everybody misses sometimes.

More practically, the common areas encountered by players who are new to the game are position play for higher runs, breaking the balls open under control, and defense.

Position play is such a complex and subtle part of the game that books could probably be written about that alone. This is where your mental processes (hopefully) kick in, selecting the correct ball to shoot next and how to set yourself up for it. You may have heard that the best players can plan their position for the entire rack in advance; if I were you, I'd forget about that. The object of pool is to have fun, not to make yourself nuts. If you can consistently plan two to three balls ahead, you should be fine, and that's true for Eight-Ball and Nine-Ball as well as Straight Pool. We'll take a closer look at how to plan your position sequences in the upcoming pages.

Here I didn't break enough balls loose, and left the cue ball in the stack. This break is usually the result of not really stroking the shot, due to pressure.

Because of the weak angle of approach into the rack, I'll really have to whack this one to get anything loose. Next shot will probably be one of the balls in the back row.

It's all or nothing here. The severe angle of approach means I'll open up most of the stack—great if I make it, disaster if I miss.

More players should leave themselves side-pocket breaks like this. You attack the rack at a vulnerable point, and keep the cue ball in center table.

Not quite as good, because the angle into the rack after hitting the object ball is too shallow. The next shot will hopefully be the striped ball at top of rack.

Where most less-experienced players go wrong in breaking the balls open is that they do just that: they slam into clustered balls with far too much speed, hell-bent on blasting them all over the table. Why is that the wrong thing to do?

1. Because all that cue-ball speed means far less cue-ball control.

2. Because clustered balls frequently need only to be nudged apart gently to make one or more of them playable.

3. Because sending your cue ball into a cluster of many balls can easily result in the cue ball's being buried in there, with no shots.

4. Because if the clustered balls are still in the vicinity of where they were originally racked, and you hit them too hard, you'll drive them out of there, when what you want to do is keep at least some of them around for possible break shots to begin the next rack.

The final five balls, all in perfect position. You can use virtually any of these balls as your break ball. Just make sure you
develop a plan that is best suited to your playing ability.

A cluster like this is going to be difficult to break up. In
this case, a safety sending a loose ball to the rail and lodg-
ing the cue ball in the stack is your best option.

Getting the cue ball into position to pocket these two balls near the corner pocket will also allow you to break into the cluster of balls in the middle of the table.

Remember, physical strength means next to nothing when it comes to pool. One of the finest players of the modern era, Nick Varner, barely weighs 120 pounds, yet he still scatters the balls with ease.

The most common error made in defensive play by beginning and amateur players is, once again, they don't think quite far enough ahead. If you don't have any open shots available, it shouldn't be especially hard to leave your opponent the same way—but that's not getting the whole job done. The concept of expert defensive play is that *you not only leave your opponent shotless, but you also make it hard for him to leave you safe in return.* Otherwise, the two of you are going to be trading safeties until they close the room on you, if you don't pass out from boredom first.

The importance of defensive play is underrated by a huge majority of all players, but experts will tell you that leaving your opponent shotless is at least as important as making

At the start of a straight-pool run, first try to clear the balls near the rail. This table offers a great opportunity to immediately pocket the balls along the long rail, leaving you with a beautiful layout.

shots yourself. Irving Crane, one of the game's true immortals and the best defensive player I've ever seen, used to practice playing *himself* safe 30 minutes a day! No rule says you have to run out the game every time you come to the table to win, although that's what most inexperienced players will try to do without fail. If you can continually "trap" your opponent by leaving him shotless, and with a layout that will give him trouble leaving *you* shotless, you'll win just as certainly as if you had never let him get to the table at all; and you'll do just as good a job of demoralizing him too. Maybe even better.

Solutions

Now that I've outlined some common problems, it's time to tell you about some solutions.

These two balls are the "key" balls. They should be saved for your last two shots, allowing you to get into position for a great break shot.

Trouble balls, like these two, should be nudged apart as soon as possible.

Normally, you don't want the cue ball to get stuck in behind the rack. In this situation, use high right English and a firm stroke to get the cue ball into the stack after pocketing the 8-ball.

Position

The first thing to consider in Straight Pool position play is that the two corner pockets nearest where the balls are racked dominate the game. When two good players get together, 85% to 90% of the balls sunk will be made in those pockets. That's why, as early in your run as possible, you want to *look for shots into either of those pockets that will clear paths for other balls into the same pockets.* You'll be surprised at how easily the table layout seems to open up for you once you put this technique to work.

It naturally follows that there's not much sense in leaving balls up at the other end of the table. Why save those? You're not going to leave any of them for your break shot (except in those rare instances when the game dictates that you must). So formulate a plan that sends your cue ball up-table to pick off those stragglers early. It will help you create position patterns in which you play from the outside in, gradually closing in on balls that have remained near the original racking area and are the best potential break shots for the next rack. The

Because you want to save the two balls on the left as "key" balls, you'll need to break into that cluster as soon as possible.

This layout presents problems because you're well into the rack but you still have balls sitting along the rail. Take care of those balls now.

best Straight Pool players always look for those kinds of position opportunities. You want to keep your cue ball below the side pockets as much as you can.

It's also a good idea to plan on shooting off object balls on or near a rail early. There are several reasons for this. Again, it's not very likely that you're going to save one of those balls for your transition into the next frame. When you leave them up there, they create the possibility for mini-clusters of object balls on the rail, which can't possibly help you. And they also clutter up paths of travel for your cue ball that you might otherwise find desirable. Even if you absolutely hate those rail shots (and many players do), take them on sooner rather than later. It'll pay off.

There is one valuable exception to the preceding paragraph. If there's a lone ball on the bottom rail (and one ball is all you ever want to leave there, in any form of pool), leave it there until you get all the rest of the balls open. The reason is that when you rebreak the balls still left clustered, it's quite possible that your cue ball will end up in the vicinity of that bottom rail, in which case you'll be quite happy there's something to shoot at down there.

I've already mentioned the importance of not moving balls that are already pocketable. It just complicates things for you, because it creates two more balls—the object ball you've run into, plus the cue ball—whose final location you can only guess at rather than predict. As I said, entire games can turn around on this, even if the contact is extremely slight. Once you get this knack into it, your game will leap several levels past players you're competitive with now.

Anytime you're considering where to send the cue ball next, examine the option of center table first. It won't *always* be the most favorable location. But it often will—because from there you can pursue shots in any direction. And it's always a good idea to plan cue-ball travel to areas where multiple shots await you. Whenever there's only one ball to play position for and you mess up somehow, obviously you're out of business for that turn at the table.

Straight-in shots, as noted earlier, aren't quite the friend you might think they are. Yes, those full-ball hits are reasonably easy to "feel" and make; but unless you draw the cue ball all the way back to a rail and then out again, you're doomed to position along that same straight line you began with. So the only logical time to play position for straight shots is (1) when they're reasonably short and (2) when they lead you to something else easy. If only one of those conditions exists, straight-in shots are a less smart choice because they reduce your cue-ball options. (Of course, if you can create a *sequence* of straight-in shots that stop the cue ball dead, that's ideal. It means your cue ball is doing the absolute minimum of traveling. But it also means you're ready for the very top levels of competition. No player ever lived who could create such patterns all the time; most of the time, the game won't offer you anything remotely that easy.)

Give yourself a break and stop trying for pinpoint position. Try instead to select table *areas* that are advantageous for your cue ball. Just how large an area will be dictated by the exact layout of the balls, naturally, but except for the very hardest racks, area position play will usually get the job done. The late Willie Mosconi, one of the two finest players of all time, used to teach position play by laying a handkerchief on the desired table area and challenging students to make the cue ball end up on that handkerchief. There's a terrific game called Target Pool, which offers you the same sort of challenge; it's so useful and enjoyable that professional competitions are sometimes staged as a sidelight attraction at tournaments.

I can't recommend you use English on the cue ball, unless you absolutely have to. The situations when English may be necessary are (1) to alter the cue ball's path off a rail, (2) to avoid hitting a second object ball, and (3) to avoid scratching. Otherwise, most of the world's best Straight Pool players do just fine employing only follow, draw, and stop-ball hits. English in any other situations will only complicate your shot, and the game is tough enough as it is.

Above all, be patient about learning position play. It's easy enough to analyze on the written page, but it's something else entirely on a pool table, and it's not unusual for players to take *years* to catch on! (Of course, those players haven't had the advantage you do.) If you try to learn too much at once, you could fall victim to what the sports psychologists call "analysis paralysis," and that's no fun.

Breaking the Balls

Far and away, Straight Pool's most critical shots are those in which you first pocket a ball and then send the cue ball into a cluster to shake some more balls loose. Not only do such break shots create your transitions from rack to rack, but even before you get that far they make it possible to run individual racks. (Only now and then will you hit a 14-ball rack and open up every single ball—and it's not much of an idea to even try; much more often, you'll have clusters to deal with at least twice in a full rack of balls.)

The most common mistake made by inexperienced players trying to open up clustered balls is to trust their luck. They determine that their shot of choice will indeed send the cue ball into the cluster, and then they hit it. That's not nearly well planned enough to be consistently successful. They should at least anticipate which ball in the cluster the cue ball will contact, and where it's going from there. When all 14 balls are racked, any of the four corner balls is the ideal break-shot target. That's because each is open on one side, making it easiest to get your cue ball into open space. If your cue ball instead contacts a ball or balls in between those corner balls, you risk getting it stuck there. When that happens you're in trouble instead of in command.

In almost every straight-pool rack, you're going to find a few balls tied up along the rail. Learn to recognize those problem areas early in the rack and map out a plan to break them up as soon as possible.

The best place for your cue ball, upon your proper execution of a break shot, is center table. So before you break the balls, ask yourself what you need to do in order to get the cue ball there. If you're contacting the top of the stack, you'll probably want to use draw. In fact, most top players prefer to draw their break shots, rather than send one ball in with follow to take on 14 others. (It's *possible* to be successful with the latter shot, but the farther into those massed balls you send the cue ball, the more you court disaster. Also, the added speed you'll need is a definite threat to your cue-ball control.) Personally, the only time I favor follow over draw on my break shots is when the object ball I've called is at least 8 inches from the stack.

Shots that offer you the chance to come at the stack from the side are the most effective. Those break shots that approach the stack from the head of the table may strike one of those top two balls too full, in which case only a lone cor-

Here's a standard Eight-Ball rack.

ner ball will emerge. I'm not crazy about breaking the balls from the rear, either, for several reasons:

- It's more important than ever to contact one of the corner balls, or else you take on the racked balls at their broadest point.

- It's hard to get your cue ball to center table from there.

- You'll be sending too many balls up-table where they can't do you any good.

Not all top players feel the same way. Mike Sigel, a bona fide great who's our all-time leader in terms of both tournaments and money won, actually seeks out shots from behind the

Many amateurs break from the center spot, but the pros often break from the rail, striking the second ball.

stack, especially for his second break shot of the frame; his theory is that center table, since it's almost always open, is an OK place to send object balls. Which only proves that pool, like all great games, does allow you some freedom to express your individuality. So practice as many different break shots as you can, and observe the varying results. Anything that works for you is fine with me.

Few players try to leave themselves break shots into a side pocket, but it's hard to understand why not. Side pockets are the widest targets available to you, and those shots represent your easiest chance of all to get your cue ball to center table; it's already headed that way. And you keep the scattered object balls at the business end of the table where you want them.

When your first break shot leaves you with another that offers you a chance to *re*break the balls still clustered, should you take that shot immediately or try to pick off some of the open balls first? Some players prefer the latter, because it leaves more of the table open to receive the balls you still have to separate. Others, like Mike Sigel, prefer to look for the trouble spots and deal with them at the very earliest opportunity. The decision, of course, has a lot to do with the specific layout of the balls. If the open balls offer a logical position sequence that will return your cue ball to that same advantageous position for your second break shot of the frame, go get 'em. If that position sequence seems too iffy to restore that good secondary break shot you have now, then go ahead and rebreak the balls.

And by all means, resist the temptation to overhit your break shots. As long as you can contact one of the four corner balls in a full 14-ball rack, a smooth, fluid stroke and medium cue-ball speed should be enough to break at least several object balls out and free your cue ball. Clusters of fewer than 14 balls can often be nudged apart to create more pocketable shots without any power at all. Hitting the balls too hard, on break shots or in general, is among the all-time leading beginners' mistakes.

Defense

The main reason most beginners have trouble learning defensive, or safety, play is that they don't especially want to. After all, the fun in this game comes from seeing balls drop into pockets, right?

I guess that's fine if all you're after is some recreation and you don't care who wins or loses. But trust me: winning the game is even more fun than pocketing balls. And your chances of winning consistently will skyrocket once you learn the right way to leave your opponent without any shots.

Here's the table layout. Which would you choose? Stripes or solids? Despite an easy shot at the striped ball in the corner pocket, I can't win shooting stripes. Notice the three-ball cluster along the rail? That's going to be tough to break up.

Rules on legal safety play are exactly the same as for shots when you try to sink something; you still must drive either the cue ball or an object ball to a rail after the cue ball touches another ball. It's also legal to pocket a ball *as* a safety, and there are times in both Straight Pool and Eight-Ball when that's absolutely the right play (of course, you have to announce "Safety" before you shoot; otherwise you'll get credit for the ball and have to shoot again). Any ball pocketed as part of a safety is respotted on the foot spot, where the balls are racked, or as close to that spot as the remaining object balls permit.

Once again, though, simply knowing what a *legal* safety is doesn't go too far in teaching you what a *good* one is.

I chose stripes, to my sorrow. (Getting proper position on the 12-ball along the bottom rail is almost impossible.) The game wasn't winnable that way, and now my opponent's solids are scattered all over an open table.

And as I said earlier, the best safeties are those that leave your opponent not only shotless but without any way to leave *you* safe.

When you come to a point where you don't have any shots, the first thing to remember is whether your opponent scratched in his last turn. If he did, you can turn the same shotless situation right back to him by merely touching the tip of your cue to the cue ball, or driving it someplace totally hopeless without touching anything. It'll cost you a point, of course, but the fact that he scratched first means he's closer to committing three consecutive scratches, which carries the

Many players would shoot that first straight-in ball for an opening shot—but it has absolutely no future. Very common error. Two clusters make stripes the wrong choice.

biggest single penalty in the game. After three scratches the player loses 16 points and has to break a full 15-ball rack as though the game were beginning again.

But let's say you don't have that edge, and there simply aren't any more makeable balls available to you. What should you try to do?

Actually, you want to try to do two things: (1) send an object ball someplace where it is in the clear, and (2) park the cue ball someplace where your opponent doesn't have a path to that object ball (or, as we say, he can't "see" it). The reason you do that is that if all you do is leave your opponent the same shotless mess you had, you haven't created anything that threatens him. For instance, if all that's on the table is a cluster, and you played safe by grazing that cluster so as not to dislodge anything, he can simply do the same thing you did. In theory, the two of you could then trade those safeties until Judgment Day; your game will be stalemated until one of you finds something to shoot at. But if you execute a safety that frees a ball or two from that cluster, and leave the cue ball where he can't get to that ball or balls, his task is considerably more difficult.

So one possibility you should always look for is a chance to roll the cue ball against the cluster just hard enough to drive an object ball to a rail, yet softly enough that the cue ball sticks against the stack. That takes most of the table away from your opponent; there is a limited amount of space where he can send the cue ball so you can't get at the ball you opened. This sounds tougher than it really is. With a little practice, you'll be able to develop your sense of speed and learn just how softly a legal and effective safety can be executed. (That's an extremely important bit of knowledge, by the way.)

The point is this: the same cluster of balls that denies you open shots can be your best friend in beating your opponent to the first open shot.

Another good buddy in safety play is distance—leaving your opponent as far as possible from the unplayable balls, hopefully on or close to a rail too. Shooting off a rail is no picnic for any player, even when there's something to shoot at. Shooting off a rail at unplayable balls, and trying to leave you no playable balls too, is a challenge your opponent may well not be able to meet.

Let's take a look at some typical Straight Pool situations that dictate safety play, and how you ought to respond to them.

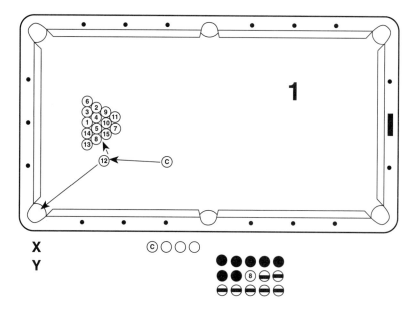

X
Y

Having set yourself up with the perfect break shot, pocket the 12-ball. Remember, one of the basic pitfalls is trying to kill the rack on the break shot. Hit the cue ball with medium speed. The balls will move plenty.

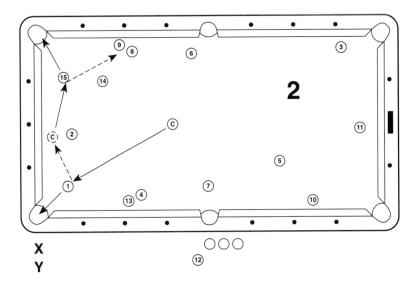

Following the break shot, you should give special attention to three areas. First, identify the trouble spots on the table. In this instance, the 4–13 and 8–9 pose problem clusters along the rail. Second, pick out a potential break ball. Here, the 14-ball would give you an optimum break position. Finally, determine a "key ball" that will allow you to gain good position for your break shot. The 6-ball, near the side pocket, should allow you to maneuver the cue ball for position on the 14-ball. Your first order of business, then, is to break up those trouble clusters along the rail. There are several options for breaking those balls. The one I would try first would be to shoot the 1-ball and float the cue ball along the bottom rail for a nice angled shot on the 15-ball. That will allow me to break up the 8-ball and 9-ball.

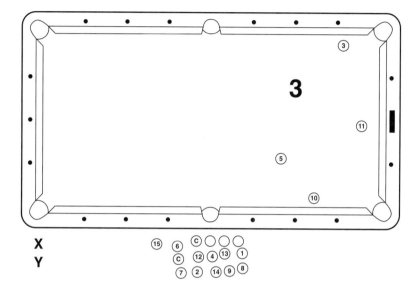

This diagram shows only the balls at the top half of the table. This is so you will understand their importance. The key in this rack is to try to save those balls until after you've cleared the loose balls and trouble balls on the bottom half of the table. The reason you don't want to pocket these balls too early in the rack is that you may need them to bail you out after you break the clusters along the rail. You're never entirely certain where those balls are going to roll. If they get tied up again, or roll into spots that make it difficult to pocket them, you can use the balls at the upper half of the table to get back into position. But don't pocket these balls any earlier than you have to.

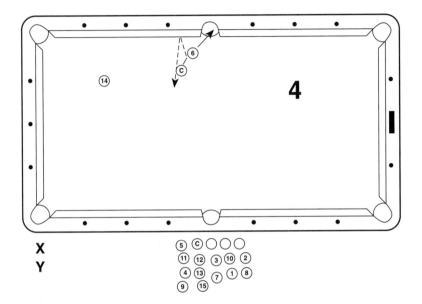

X
Y

Get nice and close to the key ball (in this case, the 6-ball), so that it becomes very difficult to lose your position for the break ball (14). Once you've mastered the sequence for running one rack of Straight Pool, there's nothing that should prevent you from stringing together multiple racks.

3

⚫ Eight-Ball ⚫

The Rules

As I said earlier, Eight-Ball is far and away the most popular pool game in the world. In fact, it's played by so many different people, in so many different places, that the rules tend to vary widely. If you're about to compete at Eight-Ball with someone you don't normally play, it's always a good idea to agree on the rules before you begin.

As set forth by the current rule book published by the Billiard Congress of America (BCA), though, the basic Eight-Ball rules are these: the 15 balls may be racked any way as long as the 8-ball is in the middle—as always—and the two corner balls are a stripe and a solid, rather than two of either one. Alternating stripes and solids around the perimeter of the rack, as players used to do, is not required today.

The other new wrinkle, a deviation from the way the game was played for decades, is that balls that go in on the break don't obligate the breaker to keep shooting them. (If the 8-ball

Clearing that solid ball away from the side rail will be important. Use the angle on this shot to bump the solid so that you will have easy access to the two striped balls along the long rail.

goes in on the break, by the way, you don't win; it gets respotted. But if the 8-ball goes in on the break and you scratch on the same shot, you lose.) Neither player is committed to either balls 1 through 7 or balls 9 through 15 until one player pockets a ball *as intended*. It doesn't matter if you make three solids and one stripe, or the other way around, on the break; the table is still "open" until somebody sinks a ball according to play. From that point on, each player must make the cue ball contact one of his or her own balls first on each shot. If a player fails to make a legal hit that way, the incoming player gets cue-ball-in-hand—that is, anywhere on the table. Three consecutive such fouls constitutes loss of game.

By playing defensively and not trying to run the rack, I left my opponent in bad shape.

When a player has cleared all the stripes, or solids, off the table, that player may then legally shoot for the 8-ball, and is expected to announce the intended pocket aloud. Any form of foul or scratch while shooting the 8-ball costs the offending player the game.

Problem Areas

Because Eight-Ball is the game so many of us played as kids, an incredible percentage of players still go at the game like kids, shooting at any and all open balls they see. The leading problem area in this game by far is knowing when you want to pocket balls and when you don't.

What makes that such a whopping problem is that it goes against nearly everyone's instincts. After all, as long as you've

Many players break from the head spot, in a direct line with the 1-ball. They feel that there's less chance of the cue ball scratching. The truth is, this break requires the most control of any. If you miss a totally solid hit on the 1-ball, by even a small fraction, you'll lose control of the cue ball. If you must use this break position, ease up on the power to gain more control.

been aware of the game of pool, you've probably thought of it as knocking balls into holes, or trying to; who ever tries *not* to sink balls? Yet far more often than you think, *not* sinking the balls will be the correct strategy for your Eight-Ball game.

Most pool today is played on smaller-than-regulation-size tables, such as you find in taverns. The most common size of coin-operated table today has a playing surface of 3½′ × 7′, or 16½ square feet less than regulation. Yet the game is still played on those smaller tables with the same number of object balls as anyplace else—and that means they're going to be bunching up far more often. Not only will the object balls be tied up, but also you have considerably less room in which to navigate your cue ball.

No matter what size table you play on, though, Eight-Ball is more complex and strategic than you probably realize. Let's

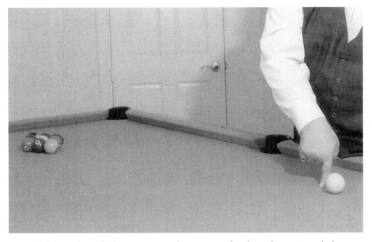

I like to break from a spot between the head spot and the side rail. Some people prefer this because they can use a closed bridge (unlike breaking from the rail). I like it because I feel I get good action from the object balls, and I'm able to keep the cue ball in the middle of the table.

While I suggest standing a little more upright for the Nine-Ball break, this is too erect. Players standing this high tend to rear up on their follow-through.

Perfect! I'm comfortable, yet I can shift some weight into my stroke and follow through.

say your opponent blasts the balls all over the table without sinking any. You come to the table and start doing what you—and the vast majority of all Eight-Ball players—are used to doing: pocketing open balls. Suppose you make five solids before you miss.

At this point, you're probably crediting yourself mentally with a 5–0 lead. In my view, though, you're down 7–2. The fact that you have only two balls left before you attack the 8-ball means that it's much easier for your opponent to defend against your getting any open shots at those balls. In other words, he knows exactly where *not* to leave you—and in addition, he has all those balls of his own that he can use as defensive weapons against you. On the other hand, you have a double dilemma on your hands: getting to your last two balls, plus trying to leave your opponent safe on all seven of his. Good luck.

So I'd make that choice between shooting offensively and defensively the number-one problem for most Eight-Ballers. Not far behind is the number-two problem, playing correct patterns once the decision has been made to take the offense. That's one reason why the game of Straight Pool is such an excellent teacher of all the other pool games; correct Eight-Ball pattern and position play utilize Straight Pool principles.

The big difference is that in Eight-Ball you can play legal position for only *some* of the remaining balls instead of all of them. Nevertheless, the same thinking-three-balls-ahead concepts apply; you want to do whatever's easiest whenever you can. You *don't* want your cue ball running into secondary object balls without a purpose. In planning your pattern, you work backward from the 8-ball just as you work backward from the break ball in Straight Pool.

Solutions

I don't know of any place Eight-Ball is played where you get anything extra for running out the entire game from the break. Yet that's what most players will try to do, every single time. Your game will improve the instant you recognize that that's among the worst possible things to do.

I'm not saying that Eight-Ball can't be won right from the break. Sure it can. But expert Eight-Ball players will tell you that the only correct time to attempt a run-out is when you're absolutely sure that you will run out the game. Not that you *can* but that you *will*. At any other time, defensive play is a much smarter option.

Suppose your opponent leaves you with the table "open" with the cue ball and two stripes makeable up-table, one near the side rail; two more makeable at the opposite end if you can negotiate position for them; and the other three tied up somehow. Instead of going after those first two balls, hoping you can come cleanly down the table for the next two *and* be able to use one or the other to break your remaining balls open, what's wrong with pocketing the striped ball that's not near the rail and then ducking the cue ball behind the ball that is?

This time you have an easy shot at the 3-ball in the side pocket. The 6-ball is sitting in a direct line with the 9-ball and the corner pocket.

At this point, your opponent can't even be sure that he will make a legal hit on any of his balls; his chances of pocketing anything are slim and none, depending entirely on luck. Even if he does make that tough legal hit, he's most likely going to open more balls for you in the process. And if he doesn't make a legal hit, and you don't like your chances of winning the game outright, you can take your prized cue-ball-in-hand and stick him right back behind the same ball.

Is that style of play fun to compete against? No. In fact, that's just the idea. Pool, remember, is mostly a mental game, and the more frustrated your opponent gets at purposely

A touch of draw will allow you to get a shot at the 6–9 combination. It's not that risky here because the 7-ball is way up-table.

being denied any open shots, the closer you are to beating him silly. Most players are used to trying to make shots. Any opponent you encounter who isn't used to resisting defense instead figures to fall apart under the pressure. You'll win far more games by outmaneuvering your opponent this way than by running out the game in a single turn.

So always be on the lookout for defensive opportunities— anytime, in fact, when it appears that you can't get all the way out just yet. What should you look to do when you're not pocketing balls? Snookering the cue ball; leaving your own object balls closer to pockets than your opponent's, especially on the rails; creating more troublesome clusters for him to solve; or any combination of the above.

Still, opportunities for run-outs actually occur during every game at some point, even if you're facing only a few balls left. However many balls you need to make in a row to win, the signs you're looking for are (1) every remaining ball has a logical, open path to a pocket; (2) you can see a position pattern linking those balls that lets your cue ball avoid all the other balls; and (3) when your run-out demands that you open a cluster to free one more ball for you (if more of your stripes or solids than that are still tied up, you should be playing defensively), you have another very easy shot in the vicinity of that cluster that you can play no matter how the balls break. In other words, almost the same conditions you look for when you play Straight Pool position.

Let's take a look at some typical Eight-Ball situations. I'll show you whether defensive or offensive options would be best—and why.

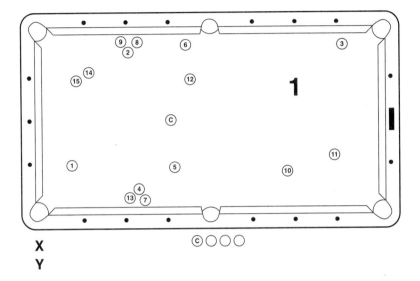

X
Y

Again, your opponent has failed to pocket a ball on the break. What should you choose? Stripes or solids? After surveying the table, I suggest you take the higher-numbered balls. Most of the balls in the open are stripes (higher-numbered balls). There are two clusters that need to be addressed. In one (4, 7, 13), the 13 is your only concern. In the other (2, 8, 9), you need to break the 8-ball and the 9-ball free to run out.

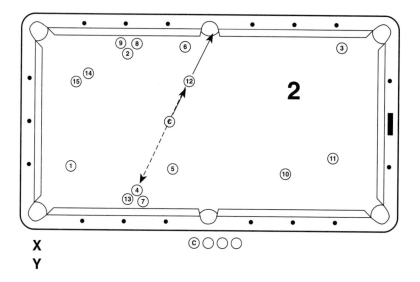

X
Y

Your first priority is to break up the clusters before you sink too many stripes. If you wait too long and fail to break up the clusters, you're sunk. In this instance, I would shoot the 12-ball in the side and draw the cue ball straight back to open the 4, 13, and 7.

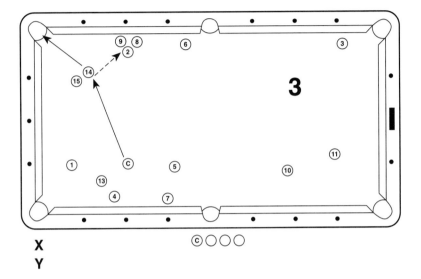

X
Y

Then, depending on where the 13-ball goes, you can choose to shoot the 14, 15, or 13. Shoot whatever ball affords you the best chance to get to the 8-ball and the 9-ball as soon as possible. If you don't get there, you can't run out. And if you can't run out, you lose. In this diagram, you've got a nice angle on the 14-ball. Take this opportunity to break the 8-ball and the 9-ball away from the rail.

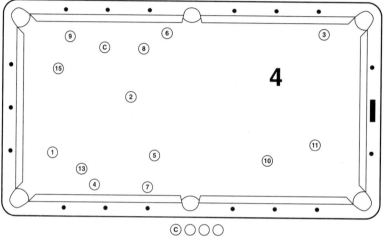

Y

Now that the 8-ball and the 9-ball are in the clear, you can pro-
ceed with your run-out. The 10-ball and the 11-ball, at the top
of the table, are no problem. Save them until the end, unless
you need them as a safety valve. That will depend on where the
8-ball and the 9-ball go after you break them up. In this diagram, you're probably best off shooting, in sequence, the 9, 15,
and 13, then shooting the 10 and 11. That should allow you an
opportunity to position the cue ball to pocket the game-winning
8-ball in the corner pocket. Above all, remember to break the
clusters before too many of your balls are off the table. That's
the key.

4

● Nine-Ball ●

If you've seen pocket billiards on television in the past six or so years, undoubtedly the game being played has been Nine-Ball. Despite Eight-Ball's status as the most widely played cue game in the world, and Straight Pool's status as pocket billiards' ultimate game of skill, Nine-Ball is the game of choice in professional tournament play.

Why? Crowd appeal! The rules are simple. The game is fast paced and action packed. Nine-Ball encourages offense in the form of spectacular shot making and bone-jarring break shots. Nonetheless, because of the game's pace and rules, creative and intelligent defensive strategies are as potent and decisive as any offensive shot.

For years Nine-Ball was viewed strictly as a gambling game. The unpredictability and suddenness of Nine-Ball—the game can literally be ended on any shot, including the opening break shot—allow players of lesser ability to win against players of superior talent. It is highly unlikely that a neophyte player could beat an experienced player in a 50-point game of

Straight Pool. And even in a single rack of Eight-Ball, a lesser player would be required to pocket his full complement of seven object balls before sinking the 8-ball to win the game. But in Nine-Ball, a lesser player can watch a superior player pocket eight balls and then miss the 9-ball. This would allow the lesser player an opportunity to pocket a single solitary ball and win the game!

Nine-Ball is also a good game for television. It can take hours to complete a single Straight Pool game (say, 150 points), and, played at its highest level, it can hardly be considered a thrill-a-minute game! Eight-Ball has far too many rules and restrictions, and it's difficult to follow the numbers and colors on TV. Nine-Ball, however, uses only nine balls, and its fast pace and dearth of rules make it visually and mentally easy to follow.

Not that Nine-Ball doesn't have its drawbacks. First and foremost, Nine-Ball allows luck to play a bigger role than it does in any other pocket billiard game. While that adds to the game's excitement and unpredictability, it may also frustrate and confound you when you play. Over the years, the professional tours have modified the game somewhat to reduce luck's impact on Nine-Ball. But luck still plays a significant role, so don't pursue a career as a Nine-Ball player if you have a weak heart!

The Rules

As I mentioned earlier, the rules of Nine-Ball are relatively simple. The object of the game is to pocket the 9-ball on any legal shot. Because only the balls numbered 1 through 9 are used, the balls are racked in a diamond shape, with the 1-ball on the foot spot and the 9-ball in the middle. The other seven balls can be racked in random order.

Since Nine-Ball is a rotation game, the cue ball must always first make contact with the lowest-numbered ball on

Here you have the 3-ball up along the rail near the side pocket. Not an easy shot, even if you try to bank it across the side. If you miss, this game is history!

the table. That's why the 1-ball is always placed at the apex of the rack. When you break, the cue ball must hit the 1-ball first. A legal break is one on which either a ball is pocketed, or at least four object balls make contact with a rail. The rules regarding a scratch on the break vary. Some rules stipulate that all pocketed balls are respotted (at the foot spot) and the incoming player gets the cue ball anywhere behind the head string. On the professional Nine-Ball tours, however, all pocketed balls stay down and the incoming player gets cue-ball-in-hand anywhere on the table. That's a huge penalty against the breaker—and a huge advantage for the incoming shooter! Why are the pros so harsh? It's just a not-so-subtle way of getting players to learn to control the cue ball on

The 6-ball and 9-ball are positioned close to the cue ball, creating a nice wall behind which you could hide the cue ball.

the break shot instead of just smashing it into the rack with hell-bent-for-leather abandon.

The rest of the rules are pretty simple. On a legal shot, a ball must be pocketed or the cue ball or any object ball must contact a rail. Obviously, if the shooter legally pockets a ball, he continues to shoot. If, however, he fails to contact the lowest-numbered ball first, or scratches, or fails to drive a ball to a rail, the incoming player gets ball-in-hand anywhere on the table. As long as the cue ball makes initial contact with the lowest-numbered object ball on the table, anything that happens thereafter is fair game. So, for instance, if I legally contact the 1-ball and, in its journey around the table, it nudges the 9-ball into a pocket, I win! Is this a great game?

Push-Out

About the only rule in Nine-Ball that gets somewhat confusing is the push-out rule, which affects only the shot following the break shot. The break is the shot most affected by

A gentle nudge of the 3-ball off the side rail and up-table allowed you to park the cue ball behind the 6-ball and 9-ball. Instead of taking a risky shot, you've turned the advantage heavily into your favor.

luck, and therefore the push-out rule was established to reduce some of that luck. Many times a player successfully pockets a ball on the break but is left with no shot at the lowest-numbered ball. That's bad luck for the breaker. Conversely, oftentimes the breaker fails to pocket a ball on the break but leaves the incoming shooter with no shot at the

A well-balanced cue is essential. To check the balance point, simply teeter the cue on your finger. A few inches above the wrap is a nice balance.

1-ball. That's lousy luck for the incoming player. The push-out allows the shooter (if a ball was pocketed, the breaker; if no balls were pocketed, the incoming player) the option of either shooting at the lowest-numbered ball or "pushing" the cue ball to an alternate position on the table. (The cue ball is not required to touch another ball or a rail.) At that point, the opponent may choose to accept the table as is, or force the shooter to shoot again. Regardless, any failure to make a legal hit on the shot following the push-out is a foul.

Problem Areas and Solutions

There is not another pocket billiard game in which the break is more critical than it is in Nine-Ball. Because there are only nine balls on the table at the start of a game, and because virtually any above-average player is capable of running nine balls, the break shot is the single biggest advantage you can have in Nine-Ball.

*A nice even layer of chalk will allow that leather tip to grab
on to the cue ball, spinning it just the way you want.*

Aside from the obvious goal of pocketing a ball on the
break in Nine-Ball, having control of the table after the break
allows you to set the tempo for the entire rack. If you make a
ball and have a clear shot at the 1-ball and an open table,
you're in great position for a run-out. Conversely, if you have
an open shot at the 1-ball and the layout of the remaining balls
suggests a difficult or impossible run-out, you are in a position to control the game by playing safe after pocketing the
1-ball, or pushing out.

The primary problem players have with the break shot is
maintaining control of the cue ball. Too often, players get all
tensed up and lunge into the shot, all the while assuming that

they're getting maximum power into the break. In reality, they're rarely generating any additional ball speed, and they usually lose all control of where they're striking the cue ball and where the cue ball is striking the 1-ball. I call it a wild cue ball. Yes, the Nine-Ball break requires power, but it also requires some degree of accuracy. The power helps rocket those nine balls around the table, and the accuracy keeps the cue ball on the table and in a position that will allow you to continue.

Problems on the break shot can be broken down into three categories: positioning, speed, and control. First of all, where you place the cue ball impacts all three categories. For a long time, players routinely set the cue ball just to the left or right of the head spot. By striking the 1-ball straight on and just above center, this method allowed players to keep the cue ball pretty much in the middle of the table. That's definitely where you want the cue ball to stay. But what we discovered was that breaking from the center didn't produce much action from the nine object balls. Too often, a player didn't sink a ball on the break and his opponent would come to the table with the cue ball sitting in the middle of the playfield and the object balls spaced beautifully around it. In pool lingo, we call this a road map. And in too many cases, your opponent is driving!

What players started to experiment with was breaking farther away from the head spot, drifting closer to the side rails. We still hit the 1-ball as flush as possible, but breaking from a more severe angle caused the object balls to rattle into the cushions (and into one another). The more the balls bump around, the better the chance that a few of them are going to find their way into pockets. We also noticed that the corner balls, which are the two balls positioned directly behind the 9-ball in the rack, tended to fly into the corner pockets. The only problem with this break is that it is far more difficult to control the cue ball. Let's say you're breaking from near the

left rail. If the cue ball strikes the 1-ball on the left side, it will slide along the rack and scratch into the corner pocket. If the cue ball strikes the 1-ball on the high side, it will simply go to the side rail and then toward the end rail. And virtually no power will be transferred from the 1-ball to the rest of the rack. The cue ball absolutely must strike the 1-ball full, which means that you should aim the cue ball directly through the 1-ball.

By no means, however, should you ever position the cue ball back near the head rail. I've seen a million amateur and intermediate players place the cue ball 2 or 3 inches in front of the cushion and break with the bridge hand up on the rail. The simple laws of physics will tell you that the velocity of the ball is greatest at the point of impact. From there it is continuously losing speed. That's physics. In layman's terms, the farther the cue ball has to travel, the more speed it will lose. So the closer you position the cue ball to the 1-ball, the faster it will still be traveling when it hits the 1-ball. And the speed of the cue ball (assuming you hit the 1-ball full) determines how much action you'll get from the object balls.

Being able to generate maximum cue-ball speed on the break shot is critical. Players think that breaking near the head rail allows them to generate more power, but that's only because they generally feel that forming a standard tripod bridge confines them and takes away some of that power. Breaking with a flat bridge on the rail simply allows you to stand more erect when breaking, and that indeed lets you use more power and generate greater cue-ball speed. But you can accomplish that with a tripod bridge right up near the head string too! Instead of getting right down over the cue and having your bridge arm fully extended, shorten your grip, stand more upright, and bend the elbow of the bridge arm. This will let you transfer more weight from the back leg to the forward leg as you lean into the break shot. That's where your power is going to increase, and you'll be able to generate more cue-ball speed.

Another common problem on the break in Nine-Ball is accuracy. In attempting to hit the cue ball as hard as possible, players sacrifice accuracy. True, the break doesn't require pinpoint accuracy, but you waste a lot of energy if you don't hit the 1-ball full and retain some control over the cue ball. The biggest offender is the player who rears his head back when he breaks. Coming up off the shot on the break is no different from coming up off the shot in any situation. Actually striking the cue ball at its center is reduced to a guess, and your follow-through goes right out the window! If need be, reduce the speed a bit. You're better off sacrificing a little power and maintaining cue-ball control.

Break aside, Nine-Ball is far more tactical than most people give it credit for being. It's basic instinct to want to blaze away at the lowest-numbered ball on the table, sending it whistling around in hopes of finding a pocket in which to hide. It's also natural for players to look for shortcuts, like trying combinations on the 9-ball that will end the game prematurely. But at advanced levels, such indiscretion is usually met with a loss.

The key problems presented by Nine-Ball are somewhat similar to those in Eight-Ball and Straight Pool. As in Eight-Ball, you have to be able to recognize when you can and can't run out. And, as in Straight Pool, you must be able to see trouble balls. Unlike in Eight-Ball, however, both you and your opponent are shooting at the same ball. And unlike Straight Pool, the rotation nature of Nine-Ball doesn't allow you to avoid trouble balls.

The thing to remember in Nine-Ball is that you are rewarded for only one thing: legally pocketing the 9-ball. With that in mind, you must always look at the entire spread of balls on the table. Learn to think ahead. If you can develop a pattern that assures you the ability to run out, shoot away. If not, learn how to turn the game back in your favor. Remember, as long as you are at the table, you control the game. And in no pocket billiard game can you gain such an immediate and significant advantage through shrewd safety play as ball-in-hand Nine-Ball. That's why over the past dozen years professional players have learned to make an art form of safety play. In the old days, safety play in Nine-Ball was looked on as cowardice. Today, aside from the break shot, it's the most powerful aspect of the game.

Perhaps the biggest problem players face in Nine-Ball is the natural distaste for giving up the table. Everyone likes to keep shooting, especially when the shot at hand is easily makeable. But how many times have I seen a player shoot at, say, the 2-ball with absolutely no way to gain position on the

3-ball? Plenty. The player figures he'll go ahead and play safe on the 3-ball. But in many cases, he gave up his greatest advantage by not using the 2-ball to aid his cause. In the diagram on page 104, you can see that the 2-ball is easily pocketed in the cornerpocket. But look at the 3-ball. It's at the other end of the table, with the 8-ball blocking it. And the 4-ball is obstructing your cue ball's path. What do you do here? Play safe.

Now, what kind of safe should you play? Should you nick the 2-ball in behind the 4-ball and bank the cue ball up-table? Or should you bank the 2-ball up-table and leave the cue ball behind the 4-ball? If a solid safety will likely result in a foul by your opponent, wouldn't you rather have the 2-ball and the 3-ball at the same end of the table when you get ball-in-hand? Of course.

Another problem area for Nine-Ball players is trying to be too precise with both position play and safety play. Remember, in almost all cases, position in Nine-Ball is a matter of "areas," not "spots." When looking to get from one ball to the next, think first about which side of the ball you want the cue ball to be on. Nine-Ball position play is about angles. Angles allow you to maneuver the cue ball from one end of the table to the other, and from one side of the table to the other. In most cases, the only straight-in shot you'd like in Nine-Ball is on the 9-ball itself. So determine early which side of the next object ball will give you a natural angle for an easy path to the following ball. Always think several balls ahead.

Likewise, when playing a safety, remember that you really need to hide only the cue ball or the object ball. Hiding one or the other usually will be enough to stymie your opponent. If a simple stop shot on the 2-ball will leave the cue ball virtually frozen behind, say, the 7-ball, it doesn't really matter how far up-table you send the 2-ball. Don't try to be perfect.

While I've told you that safety play should be considered whenever you don't see a certain run-out before you, that doesn't mean you should never take a chance on a combination that could end the game. The opportunity to end the game quickly should be measured against the likelihood of selling out the rest of the rack. In some instances, a seemingly high-risk combination is worth a chance. Let's say the 3-ball and the 9-ball are relatively close together, but not a natural "dead shot." If you look over the layout and see that the 4-ball and the 8-ball are frozen together along the rail at the other end of the table, how much risk is involved in taking a shot at that 3–9 combination? Even if you miss and leave your opponent an easy shot at the 3-ball, the positioning of the 4-ball and the 8-ball is going to make his chances of running out very slim. That's a risk worth taking.

Let's take a closer look at some typical Nine-Ball situations. I'll show you whether defensive or offensive strategies should be taken—and why.

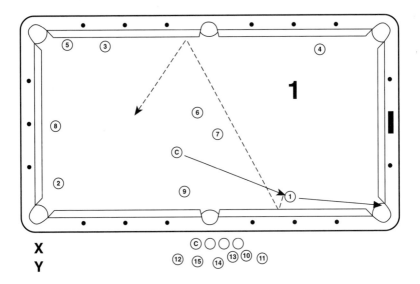

In this scenario your opponent failed to make a ball on the break. The only real problem you face is getting position from the 2-ball to the 3-ball. Where are you going to pocket the 3-ball? To gain position on the 2-ball, use low right-hand English on the cue ball when pocketing the 1-ball. The cue ball should come off two rails and stop just below the center of the table.

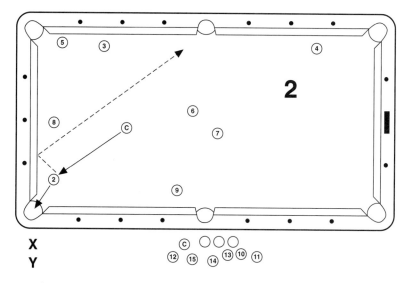

By leaving a healthy angle on the 2-ball, you can bring the cue ball off the end rail and straight back up along the rail. This will put you in decent shape for a combination shot on the 3-ball and 5-ball.

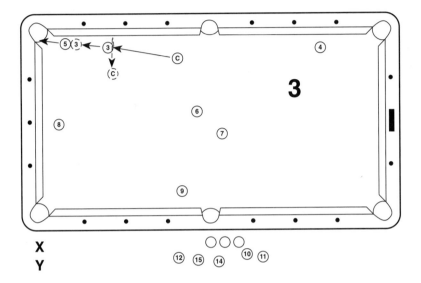

By nudging the 3-ball into the 5-ball (pocketing the 5-ball), you should be able to pocket the 3-ball in the same corner and get back up-table for the 4-ball.

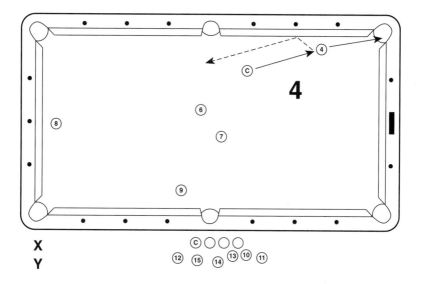

Now that you've gained position on the 4-ball, simply draw the cue ball back toward the middle of the table for the 6-ball in the side. The rest of the rack should be easy.

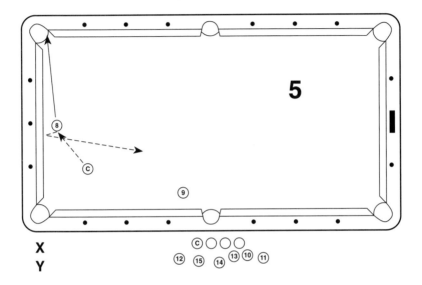

As long as you stay on the left side of the 8-ball, position for the 9-ball in the side pocket should be easily attained. You could shoot from either side, but this way you avoid having to put any crazy English on the cue ball.

Glossary
of
Terms

Angle The intersecting of two lines, which determines the desired path of either the cue ball or the object ball; e.g., the point at which the cue ball must contact the object ball in order to send that object ball to a pocket.

Balance Point The point on a cue stick at which the stick's total weight is evenly distributed. Normally, 16–20 inches up from the butt end of the cue.

Bank Shot A shot in which the object ball is driven into one or more cushions on its path to a pocket. (This does not include a ball's incidental contact with a rail, as sometimes happens when an object ball is shot along a rail.)

Billiard In pocket billiard games, when the cue ball purposely glances off one object ball and into another object ball. (Not to be confused with a combination shot, in which the cue ball strikes an object ball, sending that object ball into one or more additional object balls.)

Break (Opening) The opening shot of all pocket billiard games, requirements of which are spelled out in the rules of the various pocket games.

Break Shot In 14.1 Continuous (Straight Pool), the first shot following the pocketing of the fourteenth ball of a rack. (After the fourteenth ball is pocketed, the fifteenth ball remains in position while the 14 pocketed balls are reracked. The break shot is critical in continuing a player's turn at the table.)

Bridge The configuration of the shooter's front hand, which holds and guides the shaft end of the cue stick (see also **Mechanical Bridge**).

Butt The larger end of a cue. On a two-piece cue, the section of the cue that includes the grip.

Called Ball When playing Call Shot, the object ball designated by the shooter to be pocketed.

Called Pocket When playing Call Shot, the pocket into which the called object ball is intended to be made.

Call Shot A stipulation in pocket billiard games that requires the shooter to announce (or call), prior to shooting, the object ball he intends to pocket, as well as the pocket into which the ball will be made.

Carom In pocket billiards, the result of a ball glancing off another ball or rail.

Center Spot The center point on a pocket billiard or carom billiard table. The center point is used as a position for spotted balls in the rules of some billiard games.

Chalk A dry carbonate of lime, which adheres to the cue tip and prevents the tip from sliding off the cue ball in an undesired manner upon contact.

Combination The pocketing of an object ball through contact with another object ball.

Corner Hooked A situation in which the tip of a pocket disturbs the direct path from the cue ball to an object ball.

Count A successful shot or score. A term primarily used in rotation, in which a player earns points commensurate with the number on the object ball pocketed.

Cripple A virtually unmissable shot.

Cross-Corner A shot that sends an object ball off a side rail and to the opposite corner pocket.

Cross-Side A shot in which an object ball is banked off a side rail and into the opposite side pocket.

Crutch Another term for the mechanical bridge.

Cue A tapered stick used to strike the cue ball in all billiard games.

Cue Ball The white ball used in pocket billiard games. It is always the ball initially struck by the cue on pocket billiard shots.

Cue-Ball-in-Hand A rule that allows the cue ball to be placed anywhere on the table bed prior to the next shot.

Cue-Ball-in-Hand Behind Head String A rule that allows the cue ball to be placed anywhere between the head string and the top rail, so long as it is not touching an object ball.

Cue Tip The rounded leather tip attached to the end of the cue that makes initial contact with the cue ball.

Cushion The rubber cloth-covered rail fastened along the inner border of a billiard table.

Cut Shot Any shot in which the cue ball does not strike the object ball flush, also called an angled shot.

Dead Shot A configuration of two or more object balls, all touching, whereby at least one object ball has a natural path to a specific pocket. (The surrounding balls will not allow the object ball to move in any direction other than toward a specific pocket.)

Diamonds The decorative markings along the rails of a pocket billiard table. Used by some players as reference points for determining aim on carom, kick, or bank shots.

Double Elimination A tournament format in which a player is not eliminated from competition until he has suffered two match losses.

Double Hit An illegal shot in which the cue ball is struck twice by the cue tip on a single stroke.

Draw Applying reverse spin to the cue ball by striking it well below the ball's center, resulting in the cue ball rolling backward after contact with the object ball.

Drop Pockets A pocket billiard table on which there is no ball return gully. Pocketed balls remain in the pocket in which they were made.

English The general term to describe the spin applied to the cue ball by striking the ball off center.

Feather Shot (or Thin Hit) A shot in which the cue ball barely touches the object ball. An exaggerated version of the cut shot.

Ferrule The protective sleeve at the top end of the cue stick, upon which the cue tip is affixed.

Follow The opposite of draw. Applying forward spin to the cue ball by striking it well above the ball's center, resulting in the cue ball rolling forward after contact with the object ball.

Follow-Through The continuation of the stroke after contact with the cue ball has been completed.

Foot of the Table The end of the pocket billiard table at which the balls are racked.

Foot Spot The spot on which the apex ball rests when racking balls in pocket billiard games. Also the spot on which illegally pocketed balls are placed, as directed by the rules of certain pocket billiard games. Point where imaginary lines running from the second diamonds along the side rails and middle diamonds along the end rails intersect.

Foot String The line running from the second diamond along one side rail, through the foot spot, to the second diamond along the opposite side rail.

Force Draw and **Force Follow** A stroke that produces extreme draw or extreme follow.

Foul An infraction of the rules of a pocket billiard game, resulting in a penalty as determined by the rules of that particular game.

Frame One full turn at the table by each opponent. Inning.

Frozen The term that describes a ball resting in contact with a cushion or another ball.

Full Ball Contact on a direct line between the cue ball and an object ball. Not struck at an angle.

Game Ball The ball that effectively ends the game.

Grip The placement of the back hand on the butt end of the cue.

Gulley Table A pocket billiard table that features channels beneath the rails that return pocketed balls to a ball box at the foot end of the table.

Handicap Scoring and rules modifications to accommodate players of varying skill levels.

Head of the Table The end of a pocket billiard table from which the break shot is taken.

Head Spot A point intersected by an imaginary line from the middle diamonds along the end rails and the second diamonds along the side rails at the head of the table.

Head String The line at the head of the table running from the second diamond along the side rail, through the head spot, to the second diamond along the opposite rail, behind which the cue ball must be placed for the opening break of all pocket billiard games.

High Run In 14.1 Continuous (Straight Pool), the most consecutive balls pocketed in a single turn at the table (inning).

Inning A player's completed turn at the table.

Jaw The angled portions of the cushion at the mouth of a pocket.

Jawed Ball A ball that rattles between the jaws of a pocket, preventing the ball from dropping into the pocket.

Joint The part of a two-piece cue at which the shaft and butt ends are joined.

Jumped Ball A ball that has left the playing bed, resulting in a foul and loss of turn.

Jump Shot A shot in which the cue ball (or on some occasions an object ball) is intentionally propelled over an obstructing ball.

Key Ball In 14.1 Continuous (Straight Pool), the fourteenth ball in a rack. The ball that precedes the break shot.

Kick Shot A shot in which the cue ball caroms off one or more cushions before making contact with an object ball.

Kiss Shot An occurrence in which the cue ball or an object ball makes contact more than once. Similar to a carom shot, in which the cue ball or an object ball contacts a second object ball for the purpose of completing a shot. In some cases, a kiss may impede the intended path of the cue ball or object ball; *e.g.,* the first object ball contacted may carom back into the path of the cue ball, kissing the cue ball and disrupting it from its natural path.

Kitchen The playing area between the head string and the cushion at the head of the table.

Lagging for Break To determine which player has the option of breaking to begin a pocket billiard game, players generally lag—each shooting a ball from behind the head string to the foot rail and back toward the head rail. The player whose ball stops closest to the head rail is given the break option.

Leave The table layout after a player has completed a shot.

Long Widening the natural angle of the cue ball's path off a cushion or object ball through the use of English, or spin.

Masse A shot in which extreme English is applied to the cue ball by elevating the cue stick to a severe angle, between 45 and 90 degrees, and striking down on the cue ball.

Mechanical Bridge A grooved plate affixed to the tip of a stick which provides a guide for the cue stick on shots for which a conventional bridge cannot easily be made.

Miscue Imperfect contact between the cue tip and the cue ball, normally the result of excessive English, inadequate application of chalk, or a defective tip.

Miss The failure to legally pocket a ball.

Natural Normally associated with carom billiards, a shot whereby no compensatory English is required to achieve a desired path for the cue ball after contact with an object ball.

Object Ball In pocket billiards, any ball other than the cue ball.

Opening Break See Break.

Open Table In Eight-Ball, when the choice of a group (solid-colored balls or striped balls) has not yet been decided, the table is deemed to be open.

Peas Small numbered balls that fit into a Shake Bottle, used in various pocket billiard games.

Pills See Peas.

Playing Position A predetermined plan of action by which a player attempts to legally pocket an object ball and direct the cue ball to a spot from which he has a reasonable opportunity to pocket another object ball.

Pool The common term for pocket billiards.

Powder Talc applied to the bridge hand to assure smooth, easy movement of the cue stick's shaft through the bridge.

Push-Out In Nine-Ball, an option on the first shot following the break shot on which the shooter is not required to make contact with the lowest-numbered ball, nor force the cue ball to make contact with a rail. A defensive strategy that must be announced prior to shooting.

Push Shot A stroke on which the cue tip maintains its contact with the cue ball longer than considered normal, or shoving the cue ball forward without using a backswing. Considered an illegal stroke.

Pyramid A seldom-used term to describe the placement of the object balls in a triangular configuration at the start of most pocket billiard games.

Race The number of games required to win a set or match in tournament play; e.g., a race to nine, meaning the first player to reach nine games wins the set or match.

Rack The wooden or plastic frame used to group the object balls at the beginning of pocket billiard games. Also used to describe the general grouping of object balls prior to the start of a pocket billiard game.

Rails The top ledges of a pocket billiard table not covered by cloth, from which the cushions extend.

Reverse English Spin applied to the cue ball contrary to the ball's natural direction.

Round Robin A tournament format in which each player plays each contestant at least once.

Run Consecutive balls, games, or points successfully tallied by a player; e.g., a player may run 150 consecutive balls in Straight Pool, 12 consecutive points in Carom Billiards, or 5 consecutive racks in Nine-Ball.

Running English The spin applied to the cue ball, causing the ball to carom off a cushion at a wider angle.

Safety A defensive maneuver intended to prevent the opponent from scoring.

Scratch A foul, which usually occurs when the cue ball is pocketed or fails to contact an object ball.

Shaft The narrower, tapered end of a cue stick, on which the cue tip is affixed.

Shake Bottle A plastic or leather container used to hold numbered "peas" or "pills." The bottle and pills are used in various pocket billiard games, such as Kelly Pool or Pea Pool.

Single Elimination A tournament format in which a single match loss constitutes elimination from competition.

Slate A quarried and finished bed of stone that serves as the playing bed on most pocket billiard tables.

Snookered The inability, due to an obstructing object ball or pocket jaw, to shoot the cue ball on a direct path to the intended object ball.

Spot The decal used to mark the foot spot, center spot, or head spot on a billiard table.

Spot Shot A shot when the cue ball is on the head spot and an object ball is on the foot spot.

Spotting a Ball The replacement of balls as determined by the rules of the game being played.

Stop Shot Striking the cue ball in such a way that it stops upon contact with the object ball.

Stroke The completed movement of the cue stick in striking the cue ball.

Table Bed The playing area on a pocket billiard table.

Thin Hit (or Feather Shot) A shot in which the cue ball barely grazes the object ball.

Throw Shot Altering the path of one or more object balls through the application of spin, or English, on the cue ball.

Triangle The rack used to position the object balls in most pocket billiard games. Can accommodate all 15 object balls.

Index

About the Author

For more than 20 years, Steve Mizerak has been one of the most successful and recognizable pocket billiard players in the world. He is the holder of four Billiard Congress of America U.S. Open titles and two Professional Pool Players Association World Championship crowns, and was inducted into the BCA Hall of Fame in 1980. The Perth Amboy, New Jersey, native was introduced to the game at the tender age of four by his father, a professional baseball player and frequent patron of Madison Recreation—the city's 25-table poolroom. At his father's side, Steve saw the likes of pocket billiard legends Willie Mosconi, Jimmy Caras, and Irving Crane display their skills at Madison Rec. The youngster was hooked.

A naturally gifted player, Steve excelled at an early age, running more than 50 consecutive balls by age 11, and winning the city championship at 13. Although Steve continued to play in city and state tournaments throughout his teens, he opted for college and an education degree. From 1968 to 1981,

Steve taught seventh-grade history at William McGinnis
Junior High School in Perth Amboy. Despite his busy sched-
ule, Steve continued to play pool—and play it at a higher level
than virtually any other player in America. From 1970 to
1974, Steve won four consecutive BCA U.S. Open champi-
onships, which was considered the most prestigious title in
pocket billiards. In 1979, Steve's life was forever chang-
ed when he appeared as the star of one of Miller Brewing
Company's most entertaining Lite Beer commercials. The

60-second spot launched Steve's career as one of the game's leading spokespersons and personalities. Despite conducting hundreds of exhibitions each year, Steve managed to keep his game at its competitive best, winning back-to-back world straight-pool titles in 1982 and 1983.

Steve continues to rank among the top professional pocket billiard players in the world. In addition to his status as a touring pro, Steve currently owns and operates Steve Mizerak, Inc., distributing custom cues, cases, and accessories. He resides in North Palm Beach, Florida, with his wife, Karen.